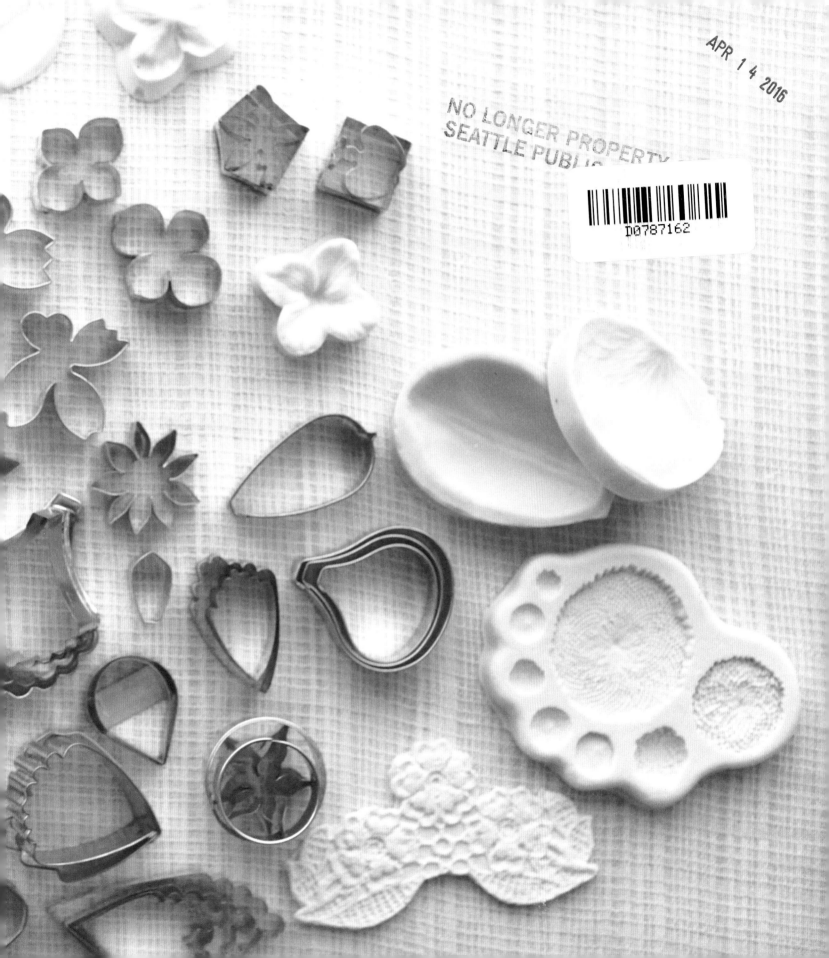

pure artistry

extraordinary
vegan & gluten-free cakes

EMILY LAEL AUMILLER

pure artistry

extraordinary
vegan & gluten-free cakes

PHOTOGRAPHY BY LAUREN VOLO

HOUGHTON MIFFLIN HARCOURT
BOSTON NEW YORK 2016

For information about permission to reproduce selections from this book,

write to trade.permissions@hmhco.com or to Permissions, Houghton Mifflin Harcourt Publishing Company,

3 Park Avenue, 19th Floor, New York, New York, 10016.

www.hmhco.com

Library of Congress Cataloging-in-Publication Data is available.

ISBN 978-0-544-19069-6 (paper over board); 978-0-544-19064-1 (ebook)

Book design by Level, Calistoga, CA

Printed in China

TOP 10 9 8 7 6 5 4 3 2 1

FOR SCOTT,

my ceaseless muse and partner.

This creation wouldn't exist without your effortless devotion and love.

contents

introduction

ike so many others, it seems, I discovered a few years ago that my body has difficulty digesting certain foods such as gluten, refined sugars, dairy, saturated fats, and artificial dyes. After restricting myself to a diet of mostly plants and gluten-free grains, I felt better. And amazingly, my allergies cleared up within six weeks! This gave me a nutritional awareness of my body's sensitivities and how it reacts to specific ingredients. As someone who bakes for a living, I started to wonder why it was so hard to find appealing foods that not only taste great but that can also be more easily processed by our bodies.

While working in the New York City wedding cake industry and struggling with my allergies, I searched for high-end vegan or gluten-free custom cakes and was surprised by how little was available, even in such a food-trendy city. While on my quest, I often asked the same question: When a person wants to serve a custom cake at a celebratory event, why should this customization only refer to the design, and not the ingredients as well? After all, the baking materials available today are nearly endless. My passion for food and my curiosity about this unknown field led to me to develop recipes for drop-dead gorgeous cakes made with gluten-free flours, unrefined sugars, plant-based fats, nondairy milks, and all-natural dyes that look and taste better than those made with overly processed ingredients.

I WAS BROUGHT UP ON THE IDEA THAT MEALS WERE PREPARED FROM SCRATCH OUT OF LOVE FOR ONE ANOTHER.

❧

I was brought up on the idea that meals are prepared from scratch out of love for one another. Over generations, my family has been involved in the food industry, from owning fresh fruit markets to a family farm to various restaurants. I've always been surrounded by inspirational people who make food out of a passion for sharing it with others. For many years I struggled because I wasn't able to eat foods that I once found comfort in. I was determined to find a solution for not only myself, but for others facing the same issues.

My first challenge was creating recipes for cakes that would have the stability needed to stack them into tiers. Without gluten or eggs, where would the structure come from? After years of testing and a lot of late-night messes, I discovered the right balance of alternative ingredients, as well as simple (yet essential) tips for handling the finished cakes to ensure success. Needless to say, adapting the tried-and-true recipes passed down through generations of my family has not been easy. But witnessing teary-eyed clients overjoyed at their dream cake has been well worth the undertaking!

I love knowing that when someone bites into one of my cakes, they are enjoying it on many levels. The first comes from the cake being fabulously delicious. Then, learning that the cake is gluten-free or vegan (or both), or that the flowers adorning the dessert are made entirely of sugar, heightens the initial experience.

In addition to being vegan and gluten-free, my custom creations are truly edible art. Just as my recipes are the result of unconventional experimentation, I also believe in the importance of experimentation and creativity when it comes to cake design. My recipes and design schemes are tweaked and tweaked again, so that each cake is designed to please the eye and palate, and always with a sophisticated yet lively aesthetic. I'm thrilled to have the opportunity to share with you my personal creations, which I hope will inspire your own culinary endeavors and beyond.

I LOVE KNOWING

THAT WHEN

SOMEONE BITES

INTO ONE OF MY

CAKES, THEY ARE

ENJOYING IT ON

MANY LEVELS.

recipes &
techniques

1

alternative
ingredients

flax seed

green tea

millet flour

cane juice

The main flours of my gluten-free mix: millet flour, tapioca flour, cornstarch, and potato starch

The ingredients you use in baking
can make a world of difference.

Subtracting the traditional basics—gluten, eggs, dairy, and refined sugars—can be intimidating. But I've discovered if you treat baking the same as cooking, using ingredients that are closest to their raw and natural form, the flavors will awaken your palate in the same way savory food will. Instead of being overwhelmed by unnatural sweetness, you'll actually be able to taste distinctive flavors in your baked goods. You'll also find that these ingredients are easier for your body to digest, and can be substituted or adjusted to create recipes that fit your needs!

While struggling with allergies, I adapted recipes that I'd known as tried and true to better fit my lifestyle, avoiding over-processed ingredients, refined sugars, animal fats, synthetic dyes, preservatives, and unnecessary fillers. On the following pages I describe my favorite ingredients and how best to use them. You can experiment with the variety of natural, gluten-free, and vegan ingredients as well, adapting the recipes that I've developed to better suit your own needs. No one person is alike—whether it's for allergies, lifestyle, or just personal preference—so take a swing at making substitutions that match your needs. Just keep in mind that altering the ingredients in recipes may change the texture of the baked good. Don't get frustrated if it takes more than one try to get the balance just right! By using natural vegan and gluten-free ingredients, you will be able to indulge in desserts that will make your taste buds leap and your body happy.

Gluten-Free Flours

Wheat isn't the only grain you can bake with! There are a multitude of flours, grains, and other substitutes for wheat flour. I find it best to not use just one non-gluten substitute, but to mix a variety to make the closest consistency to cake flour. Be cautious when looking for flour alternatives: Some starches contain traces of gluten or are manufactured in factories that produce other wheat products. Always choose products that are labeled gluten-free to be safe.

Homemade Gluten-Free Flour Mix

After experimenting with just about every gluten-free flour out there, millet flour stood out among the rest. Light yellow in color, it has a delicate flavor and texture that are ideal for baked goods. Its qualities aid in making a sweet and tender cake; I've found that other flour alternatives have a distinct flavor and denser texture that interfere with an ideal dessert profile. Millet is also exceptionally nutritious. It is high in protein, carries all the varieties of essential amino acids, and is high in B vitamins and minerals. Appropriately, millet stands front and center in my flour mix! To give it the perfect cake flour consistency, I mix it with a few other gluten-free flours, starches, and thickening agents. Adding starches and guar gum to non-gluten flours is key to help thicken and emulsify the dessert during mixing and baking, which is what gluten (and eggs) normally do. Guar gum, a natural thickening agent that is derived from guar seeds, acts as an emulsifier. You can find it at your local organic grocery store or check my resources on page 332. This mix may also be used in recipes for baked goods other than cakes, such as the Sugar Tart Dough you'll find on page 328.

Lael Cakes Gluten-Free Flour

MAKES ABOUT 3¼ CUPS | 497 GRAMS

○ ○

1 cup | 227 grams millet flour

½ cup | 114 grams tapioca flour

¼ cup | 57 grams cornstarch

¼ cup | 57 grams potato starch

3 tablespoons brown rice flour

1½ tablespoons guar gum

① Combine all ingredients in a bowl and whisk together to ensure everything is evenly distributed.

② Store in an airtight container in a cool and dry environment.

Store-Bought Gluten-Free All-Purpose Flour Mixes
Besides Lael Cakes Gluten-Free Flour, which can be bought pre-mixed online (see Resources, page 332) or mixed at home using the recipe above, a couple of my favorite brands are Gluten Free Pantry's all-purpose flour and Baker Josef's gluten-free all-purpose flour from Trader Joe's.

Flours Made from Naturally Gluten-Free Nuts, Grains, and Seeds
Almond flour, amaranth flour, brown rice flour, coconut flour, chestnut flour, millet flour, potato flour, sorghum flour, and tapioca flour are naturally gluten-free and ideal for baking. There are numerous non-glutinous flours you may use, but I find it best to bake with a personalized mix of a few different types to get the best consistency for cakes and to fit your diet.

Left to right: vanilla bean paste, safflower oil, agave nectar, sunflower oil, rice milk, and soy milk

Unrefined Sugars

You can find many of these sugars at your local shops and grocery stores. (See page 332 for a list of my favorite outlets for shopping for natural ingredients.) Liquid sweeteners are a nice replacement in icings but are tricky in baked goods because they alter the liquid level in a recipe. If you're using cane sugar in its raw form (unprocessed, unbleached, and organic), look for a fine grind.

Dry Sugars

* **EVAPORATED CANE JUICE**

   A form of sugar cane; it goes through less processing than regular sugar, which helps it retain important vitamins, amino acids, and fiber. Look for brands that are organic, unrefined, and unbleached. This is my go-to dry sugar, which you'll find in most of my recipes.

* **COCONUT PALM SUGAR**

   This sugar is less sweet in taste and has a lower glycemic index than cane sugar. Coconut palm sugar can be used interchangeably in my recipes to replace evaporated cane juice if desired. Some brands will mix cane sugar in with coconut palm sugar, so read the labels.

Wet Sugars

* **AGAVE NECTAR**

   This is my go-to liquid sweetener; you'll find it in all my icing recipes. Agave nectar is a low-glycemic sugar made from the bulbous root of the agave plant. It has a natural flavor and light texture that I've found work perfectly in icings.

   Barley malt syrup or maple syrup are also less refined, low-glycemic-index wet sugar alternatives and are interchangeable with agave nectar in my recipes.

Plant-Based Fats

When baking, fat plays a major role in the final product. Butter is often used in baking to make a tender, fluffy cake, so it is important to have the proper balance when replacing it with other fats. My preferences are healthy vegetable oils that, like butter, coat the air bubbles in the batter for a fluffy texture and add just the right amount of fat for a tender baked good. When replacing butter with a liquid oil, use ¼ cup less oil per 1 cup butter. For solid fats, I recommend a 1:1 ratio.

Safflower and Sunflower Oils

Safflower oil is my favorite vegetable oil for baking and cooking. Its mild flavor makes it very versatile in the kitchen, and it has little to no saturated fat. Sunflower oil is very similar, with little saturated fat and a subtle flavor, and can be used interchangeably with safflower oil in my recipes.

Coconut Oil

With its distinct flavor, coconut oil is best used in coconut desserts.

Applesauce

For a nonfat butter substitute, applesauce is a perfect replacement. While it adds moisture to a baked good, the pectin that it contains also mimics fat and helps retain air bubbles during baking for a light and fluffy texture. Use a 1:1 ratio to replace butter.

Avocado

Avocados are a great source of healthy fats and have many nutritional values. The fruit's creamy, fatty texture makes a great healthy alternative to butter. Since avocado has a distinct flavor and color, I recommend using it in chocolate recipes, where the chocolate will mask the avocado taste. Like with applesauce or solid fats, use a 1:1 ratio to replace butter.

Non-Hydrogenated Palm Shortening

Palm oil is a vegetable oil that is derived from the pulp of the palm oil tree. Palm shortening is made by removing most of the unsaturated fats from the palm oil, which makes it semi-solid at room temperature. When mixed at a high speed, it doubles in volume and becomes incredibly fluffy. The texture makes a perfect icing that mocks buttercream very well. Because of the high saturated fat content, I recommend using it in moderation.

Unsalted Nondairy Butters

Many nondairy butters (vegan butter substitutes) contain soy or salt. If you are sensitive to any additive ingredients, make sure to read the label.

Nondairy Milks

Baking with nondairy milks adds a nice creamy texture to cakes. I like vanilla-flavored milks. If you're looking to lower the sugar content, unsweetened nondairy milks work just as well. Nondairy milks are very simple to substitute in recipes, most having the same consistency and weight. (You can also substitute a 100-percent all-natural fruit or vegetable juice for milk. For example, I use carrot juice in orange-carrot cake and beet juice in red velvet cake!)

Rice Milk

This milk is my go-to dairy alternative for baking. Its subtle flavor makes it versatile so it can be used in any recipe.

Soy Milk

Like rice milk, soy milk has a subtle creamy texture. Because many people have allergies or sensitivities to soy, I only use it on rare occasions.

Coconut Milk

With coconut milk's high fat content, it should only be used when making a dense, rich dessert. I like to use it when making coconut cake or ganache.

Nut Milks

Nut milks are great for extra protein and flavor. The only downsides: They have a very distinct flavor and are off-limits for people with nut allergies.

Binding Agents

In many traditional baking recipes, eggs act as a rising agent, add moisture, and serve as a binding material. Since baking powder and baking soda can aid in rising, when omitting eggs in a recipe the main concern is finding an alternative binding material that adds moisture.

Flaxseed

Mix 1 tablespoon golden flaxseed meal with 3 tablespoons warm water to use in place of 1 egg. This simple mixture is my standard egg replacer and is used in the cake recipes that begin on page 73. Not only does it add protein and dietary fiber, but it helps create an ideal texture for baked goods. I've listed my other favorite egg replacers below, but would recommend using this flaxseed mixture for my cake recipes for the best result.

Applesauce or Banana

Applesauce or a banana are great additions for fruit cakes; they are a healthy alternative not only to fat but also eggs! For 1 egg, use ¼ cup applesauce or 1 smashed banana. However, when adding to a recipe, use only to replace fat or eggs, not both.

Arrowroot or Guar Gum

Both of these starch-like substances, derived naturally from roots and seeds, act as a thickening agent. Dissolve 1 tablespoon arrowroot or guar gum in 1 tablespoon cold water to use in place of 1 egg.

All-Natural Flavorings

Nearly all desserts and icings are flavored with *something*. I've explored the endless possibilities of fresh ingredients, such as fruits or herbs, which can add incredible depth and flavor. Don't be shy about mixing different types of flavoring. For example, in my Strawberry-Basil Icing on page 67, I partnered fresh strawberry puree with homemade basil-infused oil for an unforgettable cake filling. When I play around with flavorings, I'll start off by adding a little at a time until it tastes just right. Measure as you go; this way you'll know exactly how much to add the next time.

Infused Oils

You can make infused oils by steeping aromatic herbs, such as lavender or rosemary, in safflower oil. These oils are especially great for flavoring icings, such as the Lavender-Rosemary Icing on page 67. Combine herbs and enough safflower oil (or your favorite neutral-tasting oil) to cover in an airtight jar and let steep for at least 48 hours in a warm room or sunlight. Then strain out the herbs, and voilà! Refrigerate the oil in an airtight container for up to 6 months.

Spices and Herbs

Freshly grate or grind spices if possible. I find it helpful to use a mortar and pestle for spices such as anise and cinnamon. You'll get a much stronger and truer flavor from spices when using them in their freshest form. When using fresh herbs, gently wash, remove the leaves from the stems, and chop just before adding to a cake batter or dessert.

Natural Organic Extracts

Look for oil-based extracts, such as almond, coconut, and lemon, which don't contain alcohol. Oil-based extracts, made from the natural oils of a nut, seed, or plant, are much more concentrated than alcohol-based extracts. I've found that they tend to have a truer and more intense flavor.

Fruits and Vegetables

Whether you puree, juice, zest, slice, grate, or leave them whole, incorporating fruits or vegetables into desserts can be an easy way to add flair. Puree berries in a food processor to mix into your icing, or add them whole to a cake batter (fold them in at the last minute so they don't break apart). Hardy fruits such as pears and apples can be sliced or cubed and added to the batter of Madagascar Vanilla Bean Cake on page 76 to vary the flavor. Lemon, lime, or orange zest can be added to any cake batter or icing for a fresh, tart flavor. For something a bit more unusual, add passion fruit pulp to your icing, like on page 68, or toss fresh pomegranate seeds on top of an icing layer while layering a cake. Vegetables and roots such as zucchini or ginger are best when finely grated. You can also replace milk in a recipe with fruit juice for added color and flavor, such as in my Orange-Carrot Cake recipe on page 81 or Classic Red Velvet Cake on page 95. Ground dehydrated fruits and vegetables and fruit or vegetable purees can also be used as coloring (see page 27) as well as for flavor.

However you add fruit to your recipes, a general rule of thumb for measuring: When adding zest, start with 1 tablespoon; and when adding puree, cut fruit, or whole berries, start with ¼ cup.

Liquors and Liqueurs

I often add a ginger or pear liqueur to my Madagascar Vanilla Bean Icing on page 66 for something extra special. Or, before adding apples to the Sliced Apple Cake recipe on page 91, soak them overnight in spiced bourbon for a deep, warm flavor, then strain well before mixing into the batter. When incorporating liquors and liqueurs, add 1 tablespoon at a time until you reach the desired intensity of flavor. Liqueurs generally have added sugar or sometimes dairy, so consider the ingredients if you're sensitive to those things.

Fair-Trade Coffee, Espresso, and Tea

I always keep a jar of a strong brewed espresso on hand to use in baking and for making icings. Store it refrigerated in an airtight container for up to a month. Organic instant coffee can be used as an alternative, but I recommend fresh coffee or espresso for a true coffee flavor. Tea can be added to a recipe by steeping the tea in the milk called for, like for the Ganache recipe on page 69, or by adding 1 teaspoon of a fine grind directly to a cake batter, such as the Madagascar Vanilla Bean Cake on page 76. I prefer loose-leaf tea for its potent flavor.

Fresh Vanilla Beans or Paste

Vanilla bean paste is a thick, concentrated extract made by soaking vanilla beans in oil, preferably, or sometimes alcohol. It is sometimes mixed with other ingredients such as sugar, corn syrup, and/or thickeners (read the label to avoid added sugars). You may also use vanilla beans on their own by cutting a vanilla bean pod lengthwise and scraping the seeds out with the dull side of a knife. I prefer using vanilla bean paste because it stretches the pricey and rare vanilla beans farther and has a more intense flavor. Store used vanilla bean pods in safflower oil to make your own vanilla extract! I also like to store used pods in a muslin satchel in our sugar bin to enhance the flavor of the sugar. If you don't have access to fresh vanilla beans or paste, you can substitute extract, using half the amount called for.

Non-Synthetic Dyes

Using all-natural dyes in baking and cake decorating can be a bit tricky but a lot of fun! There are a handful of sustainable companies that produce all-natural liquid and powder food colorings and sprinkles, or you can also use spices, fruits, and vegetables as natural colorings. Fruits and vegetables can be used in liquid (juiced or pureed) or powder (dehydrated and then ground) form. Depending on how much you use, they can also add extra flavor and nutritional value. There are two ways you can use dyes: to dye the cake or icing itself, or to paint or dust directly on the cake or other decorations.

Almost always, if you need to dye cake, icing, fondant, sugar paste, or marzipan, you'll want to use a liquid dye to get the most concentrated color without having to add too much dye. You can control the depth of the color by using more or less dye.

Natural powder dyes, such as spices or powdered fruit, can be tricky mainly because you need a large quantity to build up a strong color, which can result in a distinct flavor and affect the texture of your product if you use too much. But if you're trying to achieve a more subtle color, such as in the Icing Domes on page 175, which get their dreamy hues from mulberry and green tea powders, powder dyes can be perfect.

To paint directly on fondant or an iced cake, mix a powder dye with vodka to make a liquid "paint." For finishing dried sugar paste and marzipan, I always "dry-dust" the decorations with powder dyes to add subtle highlights and shadows. Just like when adding flavoring to desserts, only add a small amount of liquid or powder dye at a time until you achieve the color that is desired.

The thing you must keep in mind when using pure dyes, whether purchased or homemade, is that they aren't going to match the colors in a Crayola box. Natural pigments often produce earthy tones. But there is a time and place for using artificial dyes in small amounts. When I'm looking to achieve a particular color for decorative accents, I'll use a small amount of synthetic dyes, but I do my best to stick with all-natural goods whenever possible. For special occasions, I enjoy decorating with metallic colors that are available in gold and silver dust.

Natural Liquid Food Coloring

Color Garden and India Tree (see Resources, page 332) both offer a wide selection of liquid food colorings and all-natural sprinkles.

Spices

Spices come in a variety of natural colors that are great for using as a powder for dry-dusting or mixing with a liquid for painting details on fondant, sugar paste, and marzipan decorations. Because of their distinct flavors, I wouldn't recommend using them heavily to color cakes or icings. My favorites are turmeric or yellow curry for yellow, and paprika for peach.

Vegetable and Fruit Juices, Purees, and Powders

Vegetables and fruits are not only a great source of flavor in baked goods, but their vibrant colors are useful when you want to achieve elegant shades of unusual colors. Juices and purees can be made with a juicer or food processor, but can also be easily purchased to save time. I tend to use juices to replace milk

in cake recipes, and purees in icings. When dying icings, add ¼ cup puree at a time while blending in a stand mixer. Be careful not to add too much liquid, or it will make your icing runny and difficult to work with.

Powders are commonly made with dehydrated fruits and vegetables that are ground into a fine powder with a food processor. If you already have a dehydrator, it's a fun process, but it does take time. I use these powders for dry-dusting fondant, sugar paste, and marzipan decorations and add them to icing to create subtle colors. See Resources on page 332 for a guide to purchasing vegetable and fruit juices, purees, and powders. My favorites are beets for red, strawberries or raspberries for pink, carrots for orange, spinach or kale for green, blueberries for pale blue, blackberries for lavender, and cocoa powder for brown.

Metallics

Metallic materials come in forms of leaf, petals, flakes, and dust. I recommend only using small amounts of metallic as accents on your cake décor.

Artificial Dyes

There is a time and place for accents of artificial powder and liquid dyes. For example, black, true red, and iridescent shades are close to impossible to achieve with natural ingredients.

Lemon Extract, Vinegar, and Vodka

Mix these with powder dyes, natural or synthetic, to make a paintable liquid.

Chocolate

I know I'm not alone when I say I'm a chocoholic. One of my favorite desserts is a simple bar of dark chocolate with a cup of chai tea. People who are allergy conscious should be careful to avoid chocolate that isn't in its raw, natural form. Processed chocolate can include sugar, milk, milk solids, milk fat, food starch, and artificial flavorings. Read your labels! Look for chocolate that is dairy-free, whey-free, and casein-free. Stay clear of white chocolate if you can—it isn't pure chocolate. Besides cocoa fat, ingredients may include sugar, milk or cream, and preservatives.

Unsweetened Chocolate

Green & Black's dark chocolate is a great brand.

Cacao or Cocoa Powder

I prefer raw, unadulterated, antioxidant-rich cacao powder made by Navitas Naturals, which I most commonly use when making Mexican Chocolate Cake (page 73). If you can't find it, choose cocoa powder that is non-alkalized, unsweetened, and contains no added dairy. Cocoa powder doesn't have the same benefits as raw cacao powder because it is processed further to yield a more neutral tasting and lighter colored product.

Raw Cacao Nibs

These are small pieces of broken up cacao beans. Because of their bitter taste, I use them in recipes only as an accent.

Carob Chips or Powder

Derived from a tropical pod and processed in the same fashion as chocolate, carob is a great alternative to chocolate.

Ingredients for Fondant and Sugar Paste

Fondant and sugar paste are both doughs primarily made of sugar, but they contain specific ingredients that you might not otherwise use in baking. To purchase these ingredients, see Resources on page 332.

Agar Agar

While gelatin is often derived from the processing of animal collagen, agar agar is obtained from the sap of a Middle Eastern root, and works perfectly as a replacer in recipes that call for gelatin.

Xanthan Gum

Like agar agar, xanthan gum is a plant-based thickening and stabilizing agent. In fondant and sugar paste, it works to create pliable, elastic dough.

Vegetable Glycerin

This sweet syrup is a compound derived from coconut or palm oil. It has a texture similar to that of corn syrup and gives fondant and sugar paste a smooth texture. Vegetable glycerin also helps these sugar doughs retain moisture, as well as acting as a preservative.

Gum Tragacanth

This natural gum, from the dried sap of a Middle Eastern legume, allows sugar paste to stiffen and become firm as it dries for sturdy decorations.

Corn Syrup

Fondant and sugar paste can become dried out and difficult to work with over time. To reconstitute both of these sugar doughs, add I tablespoon corn syrup per 8 ounces of fondant or sugar paste, and knead on a nonstick surface lightly coated with palm oil shortening until the dough becomes soft and pliable. I wouldn't recommend adding any more than 3 tablespoons corn syrup at a time.

Non-Hydrogenated Palm Shortening

Lightly coat your nonstick surface with this shortening before kneading your sugar doughs, both when making them and if reconstituting (above). This prevents the soft doughs from sticking.

Cornstarch

Dust a nonstick surface with cornstarch while working with sugar paste to keep it from sticking.

Powdered Sugar

Powdered sugar is an alternative to cornstarch for maintaining a nonstick surface when covering a cake with fondant without the fondant drying out. Use powdered sugar with fondant only; when used with sugar paste it adds too much moisture to the dough, resulting in decorations that do not dry thoroughly.

②

tools to
have handy

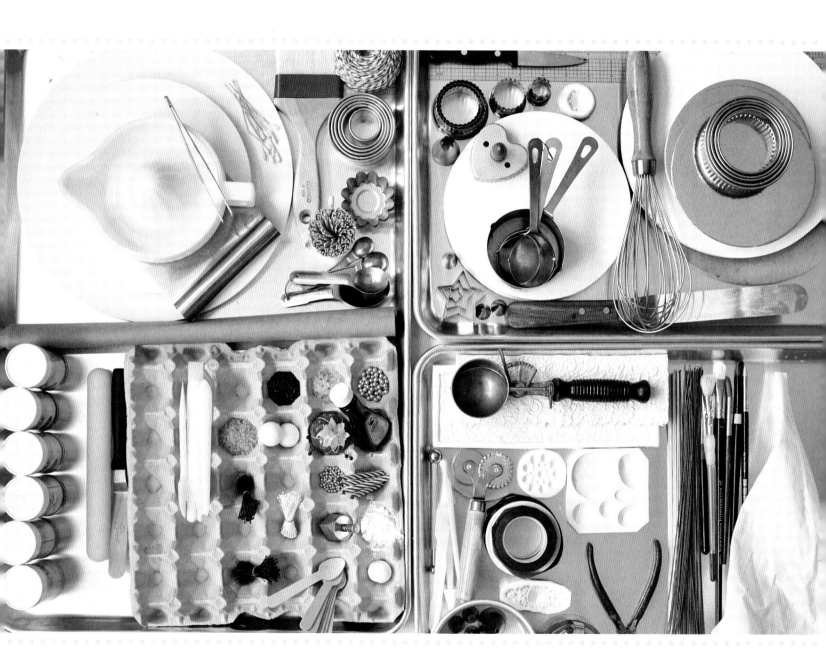

Before you start baking and decorating, let's talk tools.

Over the years that I've been making cakes, there have been a million gizmos and gadgets invented that are supposed to make the job a lot easier. Between you and me, many of them just complicate things and make your work seem mundane.

I'm a true believer in the bare bones. Because I'm a professional, throughout my career I've acquired some specialty silicone molds or flower cutters, but you don't need every single thing out there. Don't be intimidated when you walk into a baking store and there are shelves upon shelves of items you think you must have in order to successfully make a gorgeous cake. It's just not true! I genuinely believe that the creator who has less ends up with a more inventive design than one with all the fancy gadgets and tools, because it takes more imagination to create something by hand. Most of the time, one tool can be used in multiple ways, so be creative. For example, I often use pastry tips as cutters for sugar paste—both sides work great!

However, you do need to be well prepared with some essentials. You'll need different tools and equipment at each stage of the process: baking, stacking layers, stacking tiers, icing, and decorating. Here are my favorites and how to use them.

Baking Tools

Measuring Tools

You will need a set of measuring spoons, a set of dry measuring cups, and a liquid measuring cup.

Electric Scale

Weighing ingredients instead of measuring by volume is the ideal way to measure for baking. It will help you be more precise. Spend the money on an electric scale, it will change your life! (However, the recipes in this book include both volume and weight measurements.)

Saucepan, Medium or Large

You will need a saucepan for preparing specialty fillings and sauces such as Caramel Sauce (page 331), Lemon Curd (page 327), and Ganache (page 69).

Heatproof Bowls, Variety of Sizes

Metal or tempered glass bowls work great for general mixing and weighing of ingredients. They can also be used to make a double boiler for heating chocolate or agar agar, which can burn easily over direct heat.

Rubber Spatulas

Between messy batters and icings, you'll want rubber spatulas to help scrape the bowls clean!

Stand Mixer with Paddle and Whisk Attachments

I've found that with a stand mixer it's easier to add ingredients, and it will often produce a smoother batter and fluffier icing. But if you don't have access to a stand mixer, you can use an electric hand mixer.

Paring Knife

Small knives are perfect for intricate tasks, like cutting open and scraping out a vanilla bean pod or trimming fruit to accent a cake. They can also be used for cutting fondant or sugar paste if you don't have a utility knife or pastry wheel.

Scissors

Kitchen shears are used for cutting herbs and fruit for flavoring or decorations, as well as for trimming straws and cake boards when stacking tiered cakes.

Pastry Brush

I use a pastry brush to apply a light, even coat of palm oil shortening to my cake pans before lining them with parchment paper to keep the cakes from sticking.

Parchment Paper, Unbleached

Parchment is helpful for lining cake pans and sheet trays, so your cakes and desserts don't stick.

Cake Pans

When you're first getting started, it's important to have a few basic cake pans. Although cake pans come in a multitude of shapes including stars, hearts, and blossoms, I recommend beginning with an assortment of round pans. They come in diameters in 1-inch increments from 2 inches to 24 inches, and in a variety of heights from 1 to 4 inches. I use aluminum pans that are 2 inches deep and 3 to 12 inches in diameter. Because of how fragile vegan and gluten-free cakes can be, I don't usually make them larger than 12 inches. When buying cake pans, make sure to get two to four of the same size so you can bake multiple layers at once. A standard one-tier cake is usually 6 to 9 inches in diameter with two to four layers.

Icing and Assembling Tools

Cake Turntable

A rotating plate makes trimming, filling, icing, and decorating effortless.

Serrated or Cake Knife

Use a serrated or cake knife to even out the tops of cakes.

Flat Spatulas, Small and Large

A flat spatula is essential for assembling and decorating cakes. I use them frequently for smoothing icing while filling, crumb-coating, and making final coats on cakes as well as for lifting cakes when stacking them. They come in a variety of sizes.

Bench Scraper

A bench scraper is a multipurpose tool used for smoothing icing on cakes and cleaning off your work surface.

Cake Smoothers

Smoothers are specifically made to smooth out fondant over an iced cake, so you don't leave finger marks on the clean finish. They are usually sold in pairs and are made of plastic or silicone.

Sewing Pins

Use pins from your sewing box to get air bubbles out of fondant.

Cake Boards

Cake boards are necessary when you're stacking a cake into tiers or transporting it. I use two types of cake boards: unfinished cardboard rounds for assembling the layered tiers and a finished ½-inch-thick foam core board for a sturdy base. If the sides of your board are unfinished, you can use a hot glue gun to apply a pretty white ribbon around the side.

Straws

Heavy-duty plastic straws are inserted in cake tiers to distribute the weight of the next tier properly. Just make sure to remove them before serving!

Wooden Dowels

You will need a wooden dowel rod, about the circumference of a pencil, to make a tiered cake that is structurally balanced. Inserting it through the center of the tiers helps them to stay in place without shifting. You can find these at your nearest hardware store.

Decorating Tools

Muslin Bags

I put cornstarch and powdered sugar in muslin bags for dusting. Tapping the bag on my work surface controls the amount of cornstarch or powdered sugar that is distributed. Only a light dusting is needed; too much has a tendency to affect the texture of the dough. If you don't have a muslin bag, you can also use a powdered sugar shaker or a large, soft brush to dust the surface.

Rubber Gloves

When dying and kneading sugar dough, gloves come in handy for keeping your hands clean.

Rolling Pins, Large and Small

Silicone or plastic rolling pins, which are nonstick, are ideal for rolling out fondant, sugar paste, and tart dough. Wooden rolling pins tend to dry out fondant and sugar paste.

Tea Towels and Plastic Wrap

Covering sugar paste and fondant with a plastic-wrapped damp tea towel keeps them from drying out as you work; see page 134.

Cutters

I like to have a wide variety of cutters when I'm making fondant and sugar paste decorations, including cookies cutters, petal cutters, and leaf cutters in different shapes and sizes. Most baking and cake decorating stores will carry these, but you can also easily find them online (see Resources, page 332).

Double-Ended Ball Tool

A ball tool is a basic instrument with two ball shapes fastened to either end of a thin bar. When you need to shape, thin, roll, ruffle, curl, or curve your fondant and sugar paste pieces, this tool is all you need. They come in a variety of sizes and materials. I like small, medium, and large versions in seamless metal, silicone, or plastic, which makes a smooth impression in the sugar. Ball tools can be found at any cake decorating store.

Foam Pad

When making sugar decorations, it's best to work them on a durable, soft material that is malleable and won't leave an impression. You can find foam pads in any cake decorating store. Before they were widely available, I used the kind of foam kickboard that kids normally use for swimming. So, if you can't find a foam board, there are many similar materials out there that work just as well!

Sculpting Tools

This is where, I think, a little goes a long way. There are many different cake decorating modeling and sculpting tools on the market today. Some of the basic ones I recommend are a dog bone tool, a flower forming and shaping tool, and a veining and shell tool. These all have a specific use, but you can also be very creative with how you use them. In a cake decorating store, they will come in a variety pack. I like using seamless tools that are plastic, silicone, or metal. Throughout the cakes in this book, my go-to instruments are a ball tool (see above) for shaping and a veining tool for creating a center vein in leaves and feathers.

Molds

Silicone molds, available at cake decorating stores or online (see Resources, page 332), come in a variety of shapes and sizes. A few that I use often are for petals, leaves, flower centers, lace, and brooches. For flowers and leaves, it's great to have a few basic petal and leaf forms that can be reused for different shapes. I also have a flower center form with multiple sizes and shapes that I use for a variety of different flowers. Miscellaneous shapes such as lace and brooches are fun, especially when creating textures and unusual forms that would be difficult to replicate by hand.

Pastry Wheel

I use a pastry wheel for cutting a flawless straight-edge when making fondant and sugar paste decorations. It is useful when making patterns such as on the Chevron cake (page 249).

Utility Knife

A craft utility knife, such as an X-Acto knife, is helpful for making precise cuts in sugar paste and fondant.

Ruler

Use a ruler with a pastry wheel or utility knife to make a straight line when cutting sugar paste and fondant. I like to use a beveled, transparent ruler, which is lightweight and easy to read.

Wires and Wire Cutters

Sometimes you will want to attach sugar paste decorations, such as petals, leaves, flowers, and feathers, to wires. Use paper-covered wires, which come in a variety of gauges for light- to heavy-weight decorations. I use various colors for different applications, for instance white for light colored decorations where the wire would look best transparent, green for leaves or petals, and brown for branches. Heavy-duty wire cutters are used to trim wires as well as dowel rods.

Floral Tape

Green, white, and brown floral tape is used to attach and arrange multiple pieces of wired sugar arrangements. Use the color that matches the wire.

Stamens

Miniature flower centers, found in craft and cake decorating stores, are ideal for making flower centers such as for poppies and peonies. They can be attached to a wire using floral tape. They come in a variety of different colors, but if needed, they can also easily be painted with liquid dye or powder dye diluted with vodka.

Compostable Fruit Trays and Egg Cartons

You can use the paper tray or carton's natural shape to arrange sugar pieces, especially petals and leaves, so that they dry with a more organic shape instead of flat. Ask your nearest grocery store for these helpful recyclables! Make sure that they are clean and dust them with cornstarch before using.

Styrofoam Cake Dummy

A cake dummy comes in handy for drying sugar flowers on wires. If using Styrofoam that is not food-safe, make sure to cover it in plastic wrap.

Paintbrushes

I often use paintbrushes with liquid or powder dyes to finish fondant and sugar paste decorations. When dry dusting, I use a large fluffy brush; for wet painting, I use a thin brush. Keep a variety of sizes on hand for different uses. Paintbrushes also come in handy when applying sugar decorations or patterns to a fondant-covered cake, using royal icing or a mixture of corn syrup and water as glue.

To clean wet brushes, wash them in hot, soapy water, then shake out to remove excess water. Make sure to rinse thoroughly to remove all color. Always dry and store brushes with the bristles upwards so they keep their shape. If using brushes with dry powder, clean with cornstarch by gently rubbing the end of the brush in the powder until the bristle is back to its original color to avoid wetting the brushes. Keep the cornstarch in a separate container and toss it after each use.

Canvas Pastry Bags and a Variety of Tips

Durable canvas pastry bags are reusable and can be cut to use with any size tip. Use a large plain tip to fill cake layers with icing for stacking, smaller tips for decorating. You can also use the tips to cut out sugar paste shapes.

Corn Syrup "Glue"

Use a 1:1 mixture of corn syrup and water as a glue when sculpting sugar paste, and to attach sugar paste details to a fondant-covered cake.

③

cake and icing
recipes

Incorporating vegan and gluten-free ingredients
into my baking has been a test of my patience.

A lternative products must be handled in a completely different manner than other baking ingredients. When I first started writing my recipes, it often felt like I was baking backwards: I had to unravel what I knew about traditional baking and reform it into a new process. Throughout my trials and errors, I developed a lot of helpful and simple tricks that I recommend for making vegan and gluten-free cakes.

Although baking with alternative ingredients might be intimidating, in some ways it's more straightforward then traditional baking. For starters, forget the worry of creaming butter and sugar properly or the fear of overmixing a batter. In my recipes the ingredients are organized into dry and wet ingredients. The wet ingredients are generally added to the dry ingredients, mixed for about 5 minutes, and they're done. Without the use of eggs, butter, or gluten you don't have to take the tedious precaution of combining ingredients in a certain order or avoiding overmixing.

However, baking in general, no matter what materials you might be using, is a science, using a balanced percentage of certain ingredients to achieve a specific product. If the balance is off, the entire formula will be affected. I offer both volume and weight measurements because I recommend weighing ingredients using an electric scale rather than measuring by volume. It's much more accurate and will help you achieve a similar product each time. Specifically, when substituting ingredients that are of different densities, such as different gluten-free flours or unrefined sugars, I find it valuable to weigh them out, so that no matter what ingredient is being weighed, the formula will stay precisely balanced each time. Although I'm from the U.S., I almost always use the metric system (grams, as opposed to ounces) while I'm baking. It's much easier, and also easier to calculate if you need to multiply a recipe to produce larger batches.

Once the cake batter is mixed, there are a few more tips I've discovered that make an immense difference in the quality of the cakes. Vegan and gluten-free cakes tend to be more delicate in texture than regular cakes. Instead of cutting them into layers after they're baked, I separate the cake batter into multiple pans—two to four—to make the layers, filling each 2-inch-deep pan about one-quarter to half full. Then I generally only need to trim the tops to level the cakes and they're ready to be layered with icing.

If you have access to a convection oven, I would recommend using it over a conventional oven. This is fundamental advice for all types of baking, but I've found it to be particularly helpful when baking with vegan and gluten-free ingredients. A convection oven circulates the air in the oven with a fan, which bakes desserts more evenly. If you are using a conventional oven, use an oven thermometer to help monitor the temperature and lower it by about 10 degrees, rotating your baked goods about every 10 minutes. Baking cakes as close to the center of the oven as possible also helps, this being the most balanced temperature point in a conventional oven. Regardless of what type of oven you bake with, keep the door shut for at least the first 10 minutes of baking. Up to that point, the structure of the batter is very unstable, and if the door is opened, the cakes can deflate.

Now that you understand how to use alternative ingredients as well as the proper tools and equipment, and with an open mind and a willingness to try new things, you'll be able to create vegan and gluten-free desserts and sugar decorations that will not only please the eye but the palate and body too. Happy vegan and gluten-free baking!

Fondant has, rightfully so, gotten a bad rap over the years. It's known for its excessively artificial sweet aftertaste. This recipe will completely change your mind. Using unbleached powdered sugar and naturally derived gums gives it a clean, pure taste. (See page 32 for more information on these ingredients.) Fondant is great for covering cakes to achieve a clean and modern look. Generally speaking, you will need 1 cup fondant to cover a 4-inch cake, 2 cups for a 6-inch cake, 3 cups for an 8-inch cake, and so on; this recipe makes enough to cover up to an 8-inch cake. For a step-by-step tutorial on how to cover a cake with fondant, see page 116.

Fondant can also be used to make two-dimensional decorations to be applied directly on a cake. The chevron pattern on page 249 is a great example. Because fondant stays soft and will not completely dry out, it's preferable to sugar paste for covering a cake or for applying decorations directly on a cake. It will not, however, hold a firm or three-dimensional shape (for 3-D decorations that need to keep their shape, use sugar paste instead). See page 127 for more information on working with fondant and sugar paste.

Be sure your work surface is very clean for this recipe. The fondant is extremely sticky when mixing. I like to prepare a nonstick surface by dusting with powdered sugar and keep palm shortening nearby. Grease a pair of gloves with non-hydrogenated palm oil for kneading. While most cake and icing recipes work best using a stand mixer, fondant, sugar paste, and marzipan are best made by hand.

Fondant

MAKES ABOUT 3⅓ CUPS | 780 GRAMS

○ ○

1 tablespoon agar agar powder

¼ cup | 60 ml hot water

5 cups | 700 grams unbleached powdered
   sugar, sifted (use regular powdered sugar
   if you want a completely white hue)

1 teaspoon xanthan gum

½ cup | 176 ml light corn syrup

2 tablespoons vegetable glycerin

① In a heatproof glass container, soften the agar agar
   in the hot water. Let stand for 5 to 10 minutes.

② In a large bowl, whisk together the powdered sugar
   and xanthan gum, create a well in the center, and
   set aside.

③ To dissolve the agar agar, place the glass container
   with the agar agar mixture over a saucepan of hot
   water. Stir slightly until completely dissolved, 2 to
   3 minutes.

④ Remove from the heat and add the corn syrup and
   glycerin.

⑤ Pour the wet mixture into the powdered sugar well.

⑥ Using a rubber spatula, slowly incorporate the
   powdered sugar mixture into the wet ingredients
   until a wet dough forms.

⑦ Wearing oiled gloves and working quickly, knead
   the dough on a powdered sugar–dusted surface until
   smooth. If the dough becomes too sticky, add more
   powdered sugar. Grease the dough with palm shortening before wrapping tightly in plastic wrap.

⑧ Refrigerate for 1 to 2 hours before using to allow the
   fondant to set up. To store longer, keep it wrapped
   tightly in plastic wrap in an airtight container in
   the refrigerator or a cool, dry environment for up
   to 3 to 6 months.

⑨ Knead on a surface that has been dusted with
   powdered sugar before using.

Agar agar powder is used in this sugar paste as a replacement for gelatin, which is more commonly used. Gelatin is typically derived from the processing of animal collagen, whereas agar agar is obtained from the sap of a Middle Eastern root. It comes in many different forms, but I prefer to use powder, which dissolves more smoothly.

Sugar paste has similar characteristics as fondant, and is handled, dyed, and stored the same way. But since sugar paste dries out more quickly, you might want to become familiar with working with fondant before tackling sugar paste. I always recommend making both fondant and sugar paste from scratch so you can better understand the ingredients.

Sugar Paste

MAKES ABOUT 2½ CUPS | 545 GRAMS

1½ teaspoons agar agar powder

¼ cup | 60 ml hot water

4 cups | 560 grams unbleached powdered
    sugar, sifted (use regular powdered sugar
    if you want a completely white color)

1 tablespoon plus ½ teaspoon
    gum tragacanth

3 tablespoons vegetable glycerin

1 tablespoon non-hydrogenated palm oil

① In a heatproof glass container, soften the agar agar in the hot water. Let stand for 5 to 10 minutes.

② Combine the powdered sugar and gum tragacanth in a large bowl.

③ To dissolve the agar agar, place the glass container with the agar agar mixture over a saucepan of hot water. Stir slightly until completely dissolved, 2 to 3 minutes.

④ Remove from the heat and stir in the glycerin and palm oil.

⑤ Pour the wet mixture into the powdered sugar well.

⑥ Using a rubber spatula, slowly incorporate the powdered sugar mixture into the wet ingredients until a wet dough forms.

⑦ Wearing oiled gloves and working quickly, knead the dough on a powdered sugar–dusted surface until smooth. If the dough becomes too sticky, add more powdered sugar. Grease the dough with palm shortening before wrapping tightly in plastic wrap.

⑧ Refrigerate for 1 to 2 hours before using to allow the sugar paste to set up. Store, wrapped tightly in plastic wrap in an airtight container in the refrigerator or a cool, dry environment, for up to 3 to 6 months. Knead on a cornstarch-dusted surface before using.

This marzipan is so delicious you'll find yourself eating it by the spoonful while you're making it. I do, at least. Since almonds are very versatile and pair nicely with citrus or floral notes, I add a splash of orange blossom water or rose water for something extra special and unique.

If you're looking for an interactive project for children in the kitchen, working with marzipan is it. They'll have a blast molding, rolling, and decorating. It's great for covering cakes or sculpting simple figures, animals, and fruit decorations. Marzipan is a good alternative to fondant for simple decorations and handles dyes nicely as well.

Marzipan is a wonderful material for sculpting simple fruit shapes such as peaches, apples, carrots, lemons, and oranges. It takes on a spongy texture that resembles natural fruit, vegetable, or citrus. When you're done with your sculpture, take a wooden skewer and pierce a hole through the axis that either goes all the way through or only three-quarters of the way through, depending on the item. This will assist in drying the sculpture completely from the inside out. Let dry on a fruit crate for at least 2 days.

Marzipan

MAKES ABOUT 2¾ CUPS | 661 GRAMS

○ ○ ○ ○ ○ ○ ○ ○ ○ ○ ○ ○ ○ ○ ○ ○ ○ ○ ○

3 cups | 440 grams skinned, slivered
   almonds

1½ cups | 210 g unbleached powdered
   sugar, sifted

¼ cup | 60 ml water

1 teaspoon vegetable glycerin

1 teaspoon orange blossom water
   (rose water works great too)

¼ teaspoon almond oil or extract

1 tablespoon lemon juice

Pinch of fine sea salt

① Use a food processor to pulse the almonds into a powder.

② Add the powdered sugar to the food processor and pulse for about 1 minute, until a fine flour forms but does not clump.

③ Transfer the almond mixture to a bowl and create a well in the center. Set aside.

④ In a separate bowl, combine the water, glycerin, orange blossom water, almond oil, lemon juice, and salt.

⑤ Pour the wet mixture into the almond–powdered sugar well, and stir with a rubber spatula until a paste forms.

⑥ Place the wet paste on a surface dusted with a generous amount of powdered sugar and knead until a dough forms. If the dough appears sticky, add more powdered sugar while kneading.

⑦ Wrap tightly in plastic wrap. Refrigerate for about 1 to 2 hours before using. For longer storage, wrap tightly in plastic wrap and refrigerate for 3 to 6 months.

Royal icing is a staple when decorating cakes; it's used as an adhesive when making sugar paste shapes (such as the fans on page 227) or applying decorations to cakes (such as on the Beyond Polka Dots cake on page 256). It can also be used to pipe designs on a fondant-covered cake. Traditionally the icing is thickened with egg white or meringue powder. I adapted the traditional recipe to make it vegan-friendly by using xanthan gum and cornstarch in place of the egg products.

Royal Icing

MAKES ABOUT 2 CUPS | 455 GRAMS

3½ cups | 455 grams unbleached powdered
    sugar, sifted
1 teaspoon cornstarch
¼ teaspoon xanthan gum
Pinch of fine sea salt
¼–½ cup | 63–83 ml water

① Combine the powdered sugar, cornstarch, xanthan gum, and salt in the bowl of a standing mixer with a whisk attachment. Mix on low speed to incorporate the ingredients.

② Turn the mixer to medium speed and slowly add the water. The less water added, the thicker the consistency of the icing will be; the more water, the thinner. For piping or for using as an adhesive, the ideal consistency is stiff peaks; a thinner consistency is better for painting or for use on delicate sugar décor. Mix until all the ingredients are combined, about 2 minutes. Scrape down the sides of the bowl with a soft spatula.

③ Turn the mixer to high speed and mix for about 5 minutes, until the icing thickens and has a smooth, glossy consistency.

④ Use immediately, or refrigerate in an airtight container for up to 3 months. To reconstitute, bring to room temperature and whip in a standing mixture until smooth and fluffy.

Meet the mother of all icings. It pairs beautifully with any cake or dessert and makes the perfect icing for final coats on a cake! Add a teaspoon of fine sea salt or use olive oil instead of safflower oil for an unexpected mellow flavor. This recipe works best using a stand mixer. The paddle attachment is best, since it will result in a more sturdy icing for making tiered cakes. If you only have a whisk attachment, it's fine, but it will make the icing extra light by incorporating more air while mixing.

Madagascar Vanilla Bean Icing

MAKES ABOUT 7 CUPS | 1.06 KG

4 cups | 728 grams non-hydrogenated
    palm shortening
2 cups | 280 grams unbleached
    powdered sugar, sifted
½ cup | 140 ml agave nectar
½ cup | 120 ml safflower oil
2 tablespoons of vanilla bean paste
    (or 1 tablespoon organic vanilla extract
    or seeds of 1 vanilla bean)

① Place the shortening in the bowl of a standing mixer with a paddle attachment and beat on high speed for 2 to 3 minutes. Reduce the speed to low, slowly add the powdered sugar, and beat until incorporated.

② Raise the mixer speed to medium. Add the agave nectar, oil, and vanilla bean paste. Mix until fully incorporated and the icing is fluffy with a glossy appearance.

③ Use immediately, or store in an airtight container. Icing will keep for up to 2 weeks refrigerated or 1 month frozen. After refrigerating, bring to room temperature and beat in a standing mixer to restore the texture before using.

Lavender-Rosemary Icing

My husband and I escape the city during the summer by heading to Orient Point on Long Island, N.Y. We bring our bikes along on the quick two-hour train ride, in order to tour the different wineries and beaches in the area. My favorite part is the lavender fields: rows and rows of lavender that go on for acres, and the smell is breathtaking. After bringing what seemed like a suitcase-full home one summer, I developed this floral icing. By infusing oil with lavender, I was able to capture the floral aroma and taste without adding the actual flowers to the icing. Rosemary oil adds a nice earthy balance. See page 20 for how to make infused oils.

Add 2 tablespoons lavender-infused oil and 2 tablespoons rosemary-infused oil to the icing with the agave nectar and safflower oil. Omit the vanilla.

Strawberry-Basil Icing

I am blessed with a backyard at my Brooklyn apartment. Imagine that, in New York of all places! As a gardener, I had been deprived for way too long, so when we moved into the apartment, I went at it. I got a bit slaphappy, and by the end of the summer I had basil coming out of my ears. A girl couldn't make any more pesto, so I started making basil oil (see page 20 for instructions), and then came up with this one-of-a-kind icing.

Add ½ cup/126 ml strawberry puree and 2 tablespoons basil-infused oil to the icing with the agave nectar and safflower oil. Omit the vanilla.

Rose Water–Raspberry Icing

Rose water is a tonic I've always kept around to refresh my skin during humid summers, especially since living in NYC. It's fairly simple to make, but you can also buy it. The floral and fresh aroma has always been very relaxing to me, so I decided to incorporate it into a wispy icing for something extra dreamy!

TO MAKE ROSE WATER: Pour 2 cups boiling distilled water over 1 packed cup organic rose petals (rinsed and dried), cover with a lid, and let steep until the liquid has cooled to room temperature. Strain the rose water, squeezing the water out of the petals. Place in an airtight container and refrigerate for up to 1 month.

TO MAKE THE ICING: Add ½ cup/132 ml raspberry puree and 1 to 2 tablespoons rose water to the icing with the agave nectar and safflower oil. Omit the vanilla.

Passion Fruit Icing

The pulp and the seeds of passion fruit are edible, so I use both in this refreshing and tangy icing. When buying purple passion fruit to make the puree, look for ones that are well ripe and plump—as indicated by a wrinkled surface—which will have richer pulp. Cut the passion fruit in half and scoop out the pulp with a spoon. Freeze extra pulp in ice cube trays for later use. You can also use store-bought passion fruit puree instead.

Add ½ cup/132 ml purple passion fruit pulp (from about 4 passion fruits, or use store-bought) to the icing with the agave nectar and safflower oil. Omit the vanilla.

Espresso Icing

I had always been a five-cup-a-day, take-it-black coffee drinker—three in the morning, one at lunch, and one in the afternoon. Standing a tall 5 feet, 2¼ inches, there might be some truth to the idea that coffee stunts your growth! I inherited the habit from my grandpa Raffetto, who liked his coffee black and thick as tar with burnt toast each morning. When my allergies were at their worst, I started watching my daily caffeine intake, so this icing has become my special treat. By using a fresh dark-roast espresso, you'll get a true, deep coffee flavor. Stay away from instant espresso.

In a double boiler, melt ¼ cup/57 grams chopped unsweetened chocolate and then let cool. Add ¼ cup/59 ml brewed dark-roast espresso and the melted chocolate to the icing with the agave nectar and safflower oil. Omit the vanilla.

Ginger Icing

This icing kicks up the heat by combining the sour and hot flavor of fresh ginger with the pungent kick of ground ginger. Ginger is one of those flavors that will really wake up your palate and can harmonize with just about any other flavor. I'd recommend pairing the icing with any of the cake recipes or layering it with Lemon Curd (page 327) in a tart shell (page 329).

Add 1 tablespoon freshly grated ginger and 3 tablespoons ground ginger to the icing with the agave nectar and safflower oil. Omit the vanilla.

This recipe seems too simple to be true. You can flavor it by steeping the nondairy milk with herbs such as lavender, or Earl Grey tea. Use the finished ganache, at room temperature, as a filling or icing; or warm it in a double boiler until it reaches a pourable consistency and drizzle over a cake or other dessert. You can also use it to make truffles; see page 188.

Ganache

MAKES ABOUT 3½ CUPS | 794 GRAMS

2½ cups | 342 grams chopped dairy-free
    semisweet chocolate
1 cup | 235 ml coconut milk
    (or soy or rice milk)
1 tablespoon non-hydrogenated palm oil

① Place the chocolate in a large bowl.
② Bring the coconut milk to a boil in a saucepan over low heat, stirring frequently.
③ Pour the coconut milk over the chocolate and add the oil. Stir, then let sit for 2 minutes.
④ Stir thoroughly with a spatula until completely smooth with a glossy finish.
⑤ Refrigerate in an airtight container for 2 hours before using. If refrigerating for more than 2 hours, let the ganache come to room temperature before using. Ganache will stay fresh, refrigerated in an airtight container, for up to 3 months.

Scaling Cake Recipes

Each cake recipe in this chapter makes a two- to four-layer 6-inch round cake. I wrote the recipes for this size because I find it to be the perfect standard cake. If you're not making an ornate tiered cake, the following recipes can be served simply for any occasion. In order to make a different size or a tiered cake, you'll need to scale the recipes to make more or less batter. Vegan and gluten-free cakes tend to be more fragile than standard cakes; for this reason, I don't recommend making cakes larger than 12 inches in diameter. In addition, I've found that multiplying ingredients more than four times the original recipe will result in an unbalanced cake. If a larger amount is desired, make two separate batches.

Whether you need to increase or decrease a recipe, the conversions for adjusting recipes work the same way. Simply multiply or divide all the ingredients following the guidelines opposite. To make one-half a recipe, multiply the ingredients by ½/0.5 (or divide them by 2). Using the metric system is easier because there is no need to convert tablespoons to cups or ounces to pounds. Have I told you lately how much I love the metric system?

Baking times will vary depending on how thick and large the cake layer is. Good indicators of doneness are when the edges are golden, the cake feels springy to the touch, and a toothpick inserted into the center comes out clean.

The recipes for fondant and icings in this chapter make enough to fill and ice or cover a 6-inch cake. For larger cakes, you will also need to scale the fondant and icing recipes as you would for the batter.

Scaling Guidelines for Cake Recipes

All cakes make two to four layers. Servings are based on wedding-cake size slices, which are about half the size of a traditional birthday-cake slice. I tend to use the wedding-cake size for all occasions, as it's a more ideal portion size.

DIAMETER	MULTIPLY RECIPE BY	BAKING TIME (for four ½-inch-thick layers; thicker layers will take longer)	SERVES
4–5 inches	½	20–25 minutes	7–8
6–7 inches	1	25–30 minutes	14–16
8–9 inches	2	30–35 minutes	21–24
10–11 inches	3	35–40 minutes	29–33
12 inches	4	40–45 minutes	37–42
Cupcakes	1	20–30 minutes	12 standard size or 24 mini size

Chilies are commonly used in Mexican cuisine, not only in savory dishes but in desserts as well. It might sound strange, but chilies add a unique flavor to cake and pair really well with chocolate. I love a good reason to combine sweet and savory ingredients and this cake nicely balances the light chocolaty taste and the spiciness of chilies with the tang of balsamic vinegar. Feel free to omit the spices, chipotle, and vinegar for a more traditional chocolate cake with a less intense flavor.

Serve this chocolate delight when you have guests over for an unexpected surprise! For a simple presentation, instead of icing, layer the cake with fresh peach slices and a peach reduction sauce: Combine 2 cups chopped peaches, 2 tablespoons gluten-free flour, 1 cup evaporated cane juice or agave nectar, and 1 teaspoon lemon juice in a saucepan and cook over medium-high heat, stirring constantly, for about 5 minutes, until thick. (This sauce is also perfect for a cake or ice cream topper.)

Note: I like to make this cake, and all the cakes in this chapter, in four 6-inch pans. This produces thin layers that are easy to work with. However, if you don't have four 6-inch cake pans, or if you prefer thicker cake layers, you can bake the cakes in two or three 6-inch pans, which will result in thicker cakes (as shown on the opposite page); you can also bake thinner cakes in two 7- or 8-inch pans.

Mexican Chocolate Cake

MAKES FOUR 6-INCH CAKE LAYERS

∘ ∘ ∘ ∘ ∘ ∘ ∘ ∘ ∘ ∘ ∘ ∘ ∘ ∘ ∘ ∘ ∘ ∘

2 teaspoons golden flaxseed meal

1 tablespoon plus 1 teaspoon warm water

DRY INGREDIENTS

1¼ cups | 188 grams Lael Cakes
   Gluten-Free Flour (page 11)

¾ cup | 157 grams evaporated cane juice

½ cup | 50 grams cocoa powder (sifted)

> > >

① Preheat the oven to 350°F.

② Grease four 6-inch round cake pans (or other pans, see Note above) by spreading non-hydrogenated palm oil with a pastry brush or spraying with coconut cooking spray (available at your local health food store). Trace and cut out four 6-inch circles of parchment paper and place on the bottom of each greased pan.

> > >

1 teaspoon baking soda

1 teaspoon arrowroot

½ teaspoon fine sea salt

½ teaspoon ground cinnamon

¼ teaspoon ground nutmeg

¼ teaspoon ground chipotle peppers
(cayenne or chili powder works
well also)

WET INGREDIENTS

1 cup | 235 ml vanilla soy or rice milk

⅓ cup | 80 ml safflower oil

1 teaspoon balsamic vinegar

½ tablespoon vanilla bean paste
(or ¾ teaspoon organic vanilla
extract or seeds of 1 vanilla bean)

③ In a small bowl, combine the flaxseed meal and warm water. Set aside.

④ In the bowl of a standing mixer with a paddle attachment, combine the dry ingredients. Mix on low speed until incorporated.

⑤ In a separate bowl, combine the wet ingredients. Add the flaxseed meal mixture.

⑥ With the mixer on medium speed, slowly add the wet ingredients to the dry ingredients. Scrape down the sides of the bowl and mix on medium-high until all the ingredients are incorporated and the batter is smooth, about 2 minutes.

⑦ Divide the batter among the cake pans and smooth the tops with a flat spatula or spoon.

⑧ Bake for 15 to 20 minutes, until a toothpick inserted into a cake comes out clean. If there is still batter on the toothpick, continue to bake for another 5 to 10 minutes. (Baking times will vary depending on your oven and the thickness and size of the cake layers.)

⑨ Let the cakes cool completely in the pans. Cover the pans tightly with plastic wrap and refrigerate preferably overnight, or for at least 1 hour. This will ensure the cakes set up properly and be much easier to work with.

Bourbon vanilla beans from Madagascar are some of the most commonly used and have a classic, warm flavor, although you can use any type of vanilla bean paste, extract, or bean. To complement the incredibly subtle flavor of vanilla, I sometimes like to use olive oil instead of safflower oil, which adds an unusual essence to an otherwise classic cake.

Madagascar Vanilla Bean Cake

MAKES FOUR 6-INCH CAKE LAYERS

1 tablespoon golden flaxseed meal

3 tablespoons warm water

DRY INGREDIENTS

2 cups | 300 grams Lael Cakes
    Gluten-Free Flour (page 11)

1 cup | 210 grams evaporated cane juice

1 teaspoon baking soda

1 teaspoon baking powder

1 teaspoon arrowroot

½ teaspoon fine sea salt

>>>

① Preheat the oven to 350°F.

② Grease four 6-inch round cake pans (or other pans, see Note on page 73) by spreading non-hydrogenated palm oil with a pastry brush or spraying with coconut cooking spray (available at your local health food store). Trace and cut out four 6-inch circles of parchment paper and place on the bottom of each greased pan.

③ In a small bowl, combine the flaxseed meal and warm water. Set aside.

④ In the bowl of a standing mixer with a paddle attachment, combine the dry ingredients. Mix on low speed until incorporated.

⑤ In a separate bowl, combine the wet ingredients. Add the flaxseed meal mixture.

⑥ With the mixer on medium speed, slowly add the wet ingredients to the dry ingredients. Scrape down the sides of the bowl and mix on medium-high until all the ingredients are incorporated and the batter is smooth, 2 to 3 minutes.

WET INGREDIENTS

1¼ cups | 294 ml vanilla soy milk

¾ cup | 180 ml safflower oil
   (or olive oil)

1 tablespoon vanilla bean paste
   (or ½ tablespoon organic vanilla extract
   or seeds of 1 vanilla bean)

¼ teaspoon white rice vinegar

⑦ Divide the batter among the cake pans and smooth the tops with a flat spatula or spoon.

⑧ Bake for about 20 minutes, until a toothpick inserted into one of the cakes comes out clean. If there is still batter on the toothpick, continue to bake for another 5 to 10 minutes. (Baking times will vary depending on your oven and the thickness and size of the cake layers.)

⑨ Let the cakes cool completely in the pans. Cover the pans tightly with plastic wrap and refrigerate overnight. This will ensure the cakes set up properly and be much easier to work with.

What other flavors better celebrate a bright spring or summer occasion than lemons and poppy seeds? I like using lemon oil over extract for a true lemon flavor. Pair this zesty cake with a tangy Lemon Curd (page 327) and Strawberry-Basil Icing (page 67), and top it off with fresh strawberries and basil.

Lemon-Poppy Cake

MAKES FOUR 6-INCH CAKE LAYERS

1 tablespoon golden flaxseed meal

3 tablespoons warm water

DRY INGREDIENTS

2 cups | 300 grams Lael Cakes
   Gluten-Free Flour (page 11)

1 cup | 210 grams evaporated cane juice

2 teaspoons poppy seeds

1 teaspoon baking soda

1 teaspoon baking powder

1 teaspoon arrowroot

½ teaspoon fine sea salt

WET INGREDIENTS

1¼ cups | 294 ml vanilla soy or rice milk

¾ cup | 180 ml safflower oil

1 tablespoon lemon oil or extract

¼ teaspoon white rice vinegar

Grated zest of 2 lemons (wash before
   zesting!)

① Preheat the oven to 350°F.

② Grease four 6-inch round cake pans (or other pans, see Note on page 73) by spreading non-hydrogenated palm shortening with a pastry brush or spraying with coconut cooking spray (available at your local health food store). Trace and cut out four 6-inch circles of parchment paper and place on the bottom of each greased pan.

③ In a small bowl, combine the flaxseed meal and warm water. Set aside.

④ In the bowl of a standing mixer with a paddle attachment, combine the dry ingredients. Mix on low speed until incorporated.

⑤ In a separate bowl, combine the wet ingredients. Add the flaxseed meal mixture.

⑥ With the mixer on medium speed, slowly add the wet ingredients to the dry ingredients. Scrape down the sides of the bowl and mix on medium-high until all the ingredients are incorporated and the batter is smooth, about 2 minutes.

>>>

⑦ Fold in the lemon zest to ensure it's incorporated evenly. (I've found that if you add it too soon, it clumps in balls.)

⑧ Divide the batter among the cake pans and smooth the tops with a flat spatula or spoon.

⑨ Bake for about 20 minutes, until a toothpick inserted into one of the cakes comes out clean. If there is still batter on the toothpick, continue to bake for another 5 to 10 minutes. (Baking times will vary depending on your oven and the thickness and size of the cake layers.)

⑩ Let the cakes cool completely in the pans. Cover the pans tightly with plastic wrap and refrigerate overnight. This will ensure the cakes set up properly and be much easier to work with.

I created this cake one summer for a bride who wanted to offer carrot cake to her guests, but was nervous it would be too heavy on such a hot day. It was such a hit that it's now a favorite among my clients. It still has the rich, dense texture of a traditional carrot cake, but it's much lighter without the usual spices, brown sugar, coconut flakes, and nuts. Pair this orange delight with creamy Madagascar Vanilla Bean Icing (page 66).

Orange-Carrot Cake

MAKES FOUR 6-INCH CAKE LAYERS

1 tablespoon golden flaxseed meal

3 tablespoons warm water

DRY INGREDIENTS

2 cups | 300 grams Lael Cakes
    Gluten-Free Flour (page 11)

1 cup | 210 grams evaporated cane juice

1 teaspoon baking soda

1 teaspoon baking powder

1 teaspoon arrowroot

½ teaspoon fine sea salt

>>>

① Preheat the oven to 350°F.

② Grease four 6-inch round cake pans (or other pans, see Note on page 73) by spreading non-hydrogenated palm shortening with a pastry brush or spraying with coconut cooking spray (available at your local health food store). Trace and cut out four 6-inch circles of parchment paper and place on the bottom of each greased pan.

③ In a small bowl, combine the flaxseed meal and warm water. Set aside.

④ In the bowl of a standing mixer with a paddle attachment, combine the dry ingredients. Mix on low speed until incorporated.

⑤ In a separate bowl, combine the wet ingredients. Add the flaxseed meal mixture.

>>>

WET INGREDIENTS

1¼ cups | 454 grams carrot juice

¾ cup | 180 ml safflower oil

1 tablespoon orange oil or extract

¼ teaspoon white rice vinegar

Grated zest of 1–2 oranges

1 large carrot, finely grated

1 teaspoon finely grated fresh ginger

⑥ With the mixer on medium speed, slowly add the wet ingredients to the dry ingredients. Scrape down the sides of the bowl and mix on medium-high until all the ingredients are incorporated and the batter is smooth, about 2 minutes.

⑦ Fold in the orange zest, carrot, and ginger to ensure they are evenly incorporated. (I've found that if you add these ingredients any sooner, they clump in balls.)

⑧ Divide the batter among the cake pans and smooth the tops with a flat spatula or spoon.

⑨ Bake for about 20 minutes, until a toothpick inserted into one of the cakes comes out clean. If there is still batter on the toothpick, continue to bake for another 5 to 10 minutes. (Baking times will vary depending on your oven and the thickness and size of the cake layers.)

⑩ Let the cakes cool completely in the pans. Cover the pans tightly with plastic wrap and refrigerate overnight. This will ensure the cakes set up properly and be much easier to work with.

One of my earliest memories of coconut as a child was when my mom took my sister and me, once in a blue moon, to the Hostess store downtown to pick up a treat. We always went for Sno Balls, the coconut marshmallow–covered chocolate cake with a creamy filling. Depending on the season, sometimes you could find them in pink—which I thought was the coolest thing. As an adult, this cake is probably the closest thing that I will ever come to another Hostess Sno Ball. For nostalgic purposes, I like to layer it with Ganache (page 69) and top it off with Madagascar Vanilla Bean Icing (page 66) and toasted coconut flakes.

Coconut Cake

MAKES FOUR 6-INCH CAKE LAYERS

. . . .

1 tablespoon golden flaxseed meal

3 tablespoons warm water

DRY INGREDIENTS

2 cups | 300 grams Lael Cakes
   Gluten-Free Flour (page 11)

1 cup | 210 grams evaporated cane juice

½ cup | 25 grams unsweetened coconut
   flakes (use sweetened coconut flakes if
   you like your cakes on the sweeter side)

1 teaspoon baking soda

1 teaspoon baking powder

1 teaspoon arrowroot

½ teaspoon fine sea salt

>>>

① Preheat the oven to 350°F.

② Grease four 6-inch round cake pans (or other pans, see Note on page 73) by spreading non-hydrogenated palm shortening with a pastry brush or spraying with coconut cooking spray (available at your local health food store). Trace and cut out four 6-inch circles of parchment paper and place on the bottom of each greased pan.

③ In a small bowl, combine the flaxseed meal and warm water. Set aside.

④ In the bowl of a standing mixer with a paddle attachment, combine the dry ingredients. Mix on low speed until incorporated.

⑤ In a separate bowl, combine the wet ingredients. Add the flaxseed meal mixture.

>>>

WET INGREDIENTS

1¼ cups | 294 ml coconut milk

¾ cup | 180 ml safflower oil

1 tablespoon coconut flavor or extract

¼ teaspoon white rice vinegar

¼ cup | 12 grams coconut flakes or
  shredded coconut, for garnish (optional)

⑥ With the mixer on medium speed, slowly add the wet ingredients to the dry ingredients. Scrape down the sides of the bowl and mix on medium-high until all the ingredients are incorporated and the batter is smooth, about 2 minutes.

⑦ Divide the batter among the cake pans and smooth the tops with a flat spatula or spoon.

⑧ Bake for about 20 minutes, until a toothpick inserted in one of the cakes comes out clean. If there is still batter on the toothpick, continue to bake for another 5 to 10 minutes. (Baking times will vary depending on your oven and the thickness and size of the cake layers.)

⑨ Let the cakes cool completely in the pans. Cover the pans tightly with plastic wrap and refrigerate overnight. This will ensure the cakes set up properly and be much easier to work with.

⑩ Garnish with the cocout flakes when serving, if desired.

I'm a ginger fanatic, so I kicked up the ginger an extra notch in this recipe. You can add even more fresh ginger if you're a huge fan. You could also toss in a tablespoon of ginger syrup for extra bite. (Buy ginger syrup at a gourmet store or make it; it's just ginger-flavored simple syrup: Simmer equal parts sugar and water with some peeled fresh ginger, using 6 to 8 large pieces for every 1 cup of sugar. After the sugar has dissolved, carefully remove the ginger pieces and let the syrup cool completely before refrigerating in an airtight container for up to 6 months.) Pair the cake with a fresh, light icing, such as the Passion Fruit Icing on page 68.

Ginger Cake

MAKES FOUR 6-INCH CAKE LAYERS

. . . .

1 tablespoon golden flaxseed meal

3 tablespoons warm water

DRY INGREDIENTS

2 cups | 300 grams Lael Cakes
   Gluten-Free Flour (page 11)

1 cup | 210 grams evaporated cane juice

2 tablespoons finely grated fresh ginger

2 teaspoons ground ginger

1 teaspoon baking soda

1 teaspoon baking powder

1 teaspoon arrowroot

½ teaspoon fine sea salt

>>>

① Preheat the oven to 350°F.

② Grease four 6-inch round cake pans (or other pans, see Note on page 73) by spreading non-hydrogenated palm shortening with a pastry brush or spraying with coconut cooking spray (available at your local health food store). Trace and cut out four 6-inch circles of parchment paper and place on the bottom of each greased pan.

③ In a small bowl, combine the flaxseed meal and warm water. Set aside.

④ In the bowl of a standing mixer with a paddle attachment, combine the dry ingredients. Mix on low speed until incorporated.

⑤ In a separate bowl, combine the wet ingredients. Add the flaxseed meal mixture.

>>>

WET INGREDIENTS

1¼ cups | 294 ml vanilla soy or rice milk

¾ cup | 180 ml safflower oil

¼ teaspoon white rice vinegar

⑥ With the mixer on medium speed, slowly add the wet ingredients to the dry ingredients. Scrape down the sides of the bowl and mix on medium-high until all the ingredients are incorporated and the batter is smooth, about 2 minutes.

⑦ Divide the batter among the cake pans and smooth the tops with a flat spatula or spoon.

⑧ Bake for about 20 minutes, until a toothpick inserted in one of the cakes comes out clean. If there is still batter on the toothpick, continue to bake for another 5 to 10 minutes. (Baking times will vary depending on your oven and the thickness and size of the cake layers.)

⑨ Let the cakes cool completely in the pans. Cover the pans tightly with plastic wrap and refrigerate overnight. This will ensure the cakes set up properly and be much easier to work with.

There's nothing better than the aroma of baked apples filling the kitchen. This is my version of an apple pie in the form of a cake, if that's possible. I like to use Honeycrisp or Pink Lady apples when baking. For extra spice, add more freshly grated ginger; as I mention in the Ginger Cake recipe (page 89), I love ginger! If you're feeling ambitious, pour fresh Caramel Sauce (page 331) over the top and serve with a scoop of vanilla bean sorbet.

Sliced Apple Cake

MAKES FOUR 6-INCH CAKE LAYERS

1 tablespoon golden flaxseed meal

3 tablespoons warm water

1 apple, peeled, cored, and sliced

1 tablespoon lemon juice

3 tablespoons evaporated cane juice

DRY INGREDIENTS

2 cups | 300 grams Lael Cakes
　　Gluten-Free Flour (page 11)

1 cup | 210 grams evaporated cane juice

1 teaspoon baking soda

1 teaspoon baking powder

1 teaspoon arrowroot

1 teaspoon ground cinnamon

½ teaspoon freshly grated nutmeg

½ teaspoon fine sea salt

>>>

① Preheat the oven to 350°F.

② Grease four 6-inch round cake pans (or other pans, see Note on page 73) by spreading non-hydrogenated palm shortening with a pastry brush or spraying with coconut cooking spray (available at your local health food store). Trace and cut out four 6-inch circles of parchment paper and place on the bottom of each greased pan.

③ In a small bowl, combine the flaxseed meal and warm water. Set aside.

④ In a separate bowl, combine the apple slices, lemon juice, and the 3 tablespoons evaporated cane juice. Set aside.

⑤ In the bowl of a standing mixer with a paddle attachment, combine the dry ingredients. Mix on low speed until incorporated.

>>>

WET INGREDIENTS

1¼ cups | 294 ml vanilla soy or rice milk

1 tablespoon vanilla bean paste
   (or ½ tablespoon organic vanilla extract
   or seeds of 1 vanilla bean)

¾ cup | 180 ml safflower oil

1 tablespoon finely grated fresh ginger

¼ teaspoon white rice vinegar

⑥ In a separate bowl, combine the wet ingredients. Add the flaxseed meal mixture.

⑦ With the mixer on medium speed, slowly add the wet ingredients to the dry ingredients. Scrape down the sides of the bowl and mix on medium-high until all the ingredients are incorporated and the batter is smooth, about 2 minutes.

⑧ Fold in the apple mixture; adding them last helps the apples hold their shape nicely.

⑨ Divide the batter among the cake pans and smooth the tops with a flat spatula or spoon.

⑩ Bake for about 20 minutes, until a toothpick inserted in one of the cakes comes out clean. If there is still batter on the toothpick, continue to bake for another 5 to 10 minutes. (Baking times will vary depending on your oven and the thickness and size of the cake layers.)

⑪ Let the cakes cool completely in the pans. Cover the pans tightly with plastic wrap and refrigerate overnight. This will ensure the cakes set up properly and be much easier to work with.

Okay, so I have a confession to make: I never really "got" red velvet cake. I mean, I get that it's bright and pretty. Beyond the color, though, it's hard to pinpoint what makes it appealing to so many people. Because of my allergies to artificial dyes, I dug deeper into the history of red velvet—there had to be more to it than just a boatload of red food coloring—and discovered the genesis of this moist, lightly-flavored cake.

Before alkaline "Dutch processed" cocoa was widely available, cocoa powder naturally had a red tint, which became associated with this beloved cake. Artificial dye was eventually added to the recipe to enhance this red color. However, some bakers have been known to incorporate beets instead. Now, I can get down with beets! In this recipe, I use beet powder (ground dehydrated beets; see Resources on page 332 for purchasing information) and beet juice for color and moisture. But I do cheat a little, too, by using an all-natural red food coloring to pump up the red. Not only does this cake emerge from the oven with a luxurious maroon hue, but the flavor complexity is beyond comparison.

Classic Red Velvet Cake

MAKES FOUR 6-INCH CAKE LAYERS

○ ○ ○ ○ ○ ○ ○ ○ ○ ○ ○ ○ ○ ○ ○ ○ ○ ○ ○

1 tablespoon golden flaxseed meal

3 tablespoons warm water

DRY INGREDIENTS

1¾ cups | 300 grams Lael Cakes
    Gluten-Free Flour (page 11)

1 cup | 210 grams evaporated cane juice

¼ cup | 25 grams cocoa powder

2 tablespoons beet powder

1 teaspoon baking soda

1 teaspoon baking powder

1 teaspoon arrowroot

½ teaspoon fine sea salt

>>>

① Preheat the oven to 350°F.

② Grease four 6-inch round cake pans (or other pans, see Note on page 73) by spreading non-hydrogenated palm shortening with a pastry brush or spraying with coconut cooking spray (available at your local health food store). Trace and cut out four 6-inch circles of parchment paper and place on the bottom of each greased pan.

③ In a small bowl, combine the flaxseed meal and warm water. Set aside.

>>>

WET INGREDIENTS

1½ cups | 356 ml beet juice

¾ cup | 180 ml safflower oil

3 tablespoons all-natural red food coloring

1 tablespoon vanilla bean paste
   (or ½ tablespoon organic vanilla extract
   or seeds of 1 vanilla bean)

½ teaspoon white rice vinegar

④ In the bowl of a standing mixer with a paddle attachment, combine the dry ingredients. Mix on low speed until incorporated.

⑤ In a separate bowl, combine the wet ingredients. Add the flaxseed meal mixture.

⑥ With the mixer on medium speed, slowly add the wet ingredients to the dry ingredients. Scrape down the sides of the bowl and mix on medium-high until all the ingredients are incorporated and the batter is smooth, about 2 minutes.

⑦ Divide the batter among the cake pans and smooth the tops with a flat spatula or spoon.

⑧ Bake for about 20 minutes, until a toothpick inserted in one of the cakes comes out clean. If there is still batter on the toothpick, continue to bake for another 5 to 10 minutes. (Baking times will vary depending on your oven and the thickness and size of the cake layers.)

⑨ Let the cakes cool completely in the pans. Cover the pans tightly with plastic wrap and refrigerate overnight. This will ensure the cakes set up properly and be much easier to work with.

4

cake construction

Considering how much thought and effort will go
into decorating the exterior of a cake,
it's crucial to have the interior properly assembled
so that you have a sound structure—especially
when making a tiered cake.

You *can use* the following techniques for a small, simple layer cake or a large tiered cake. Either way, I recommend using a turntable.

When you're building, layering, and stacking a cake it takes concentration and precision to be successful. These steps will need your patience and consistency the most. Once you've iced and stacked your cake to its desired height and shape, you can then decorate it! If you've followed these steps carefully, decorating will seem easy breezy.

Removing a Cake from the Pan

Since vegan, gluten-free cakes are particularly fragile, I find it helpful to keep each cake layer on a separate board while working with them. This ensures that the structure of the cake stays stable for stacking and tiering.

TOOLS:

• 2 cardboard cake rounds per cake pan, equivalent to or slightly larger than the size of the cake pans

❶ Place a cardboard cake board on top of the cake pan and carefully turn the pan over.

❷ Gently tap the pan against the work surface until the cake comes loose, then remove the pan.

❸ Remove the parchment paper from the bottom of the cake.

❹ Place the second cake board over the bottom of the cake.

❺ Flip the cake over so that it's right side up and remove the top board.

Trimming a Cake

After you remove the cake layers from the pans, it is important that you trim the cake tops to make a level, even layer before filling and icing. This will help ensure an even and stable layered cake. Traditional cakes are often sliced horizontally to make multiple layers, but I don't recommend doing that with vegan, gluten-free cakes because they are much more fragile than traditional cakes.

TOOLS:
- cake turntable
- serrated knife

❶ Place the cake board with the cake layer on a turntable. Use a serrated cake knife to carefully trim excess cake off the top to create an even, level surface.

❷ Repeat this step for all cake layers before filling.

Preparing a Pastry Bag

I wouldn't be able to live without pastry bags in my kitchen. I use them for making desserts, such as the truffles on page 188, filling cakes with icing, and decorating. I often use canvas bags, which are reusable and easy to clean.

Icing can be used beyond filling and coating a cake. With a pastry bag and different piping tips, you can decorate a cake with decorative icing. See Chapter 6 for examples of two different styles of piping that use round tips: simple piped domes created with a large round tip (page 175) and a more intricate piped design made with a small round tip (page 180). Pastry bags and piping tips are also great for decorating cupcakes and petite desserts, such as the filled tarts and piped cupcakes shown on pages 312 to 321, which were made using multiple sizes of round and star tips.

TOOLS:

• canvas pastry bag

• pastry tip(s)

• scissors

❶ Fold the top of the pastry bag out to help keep filling from getting on the outside of the bag.

② From the inside of the bag, drop the piping tip into the opening (you may need to trim the opening with scissors to fit the appropriate tip size) and adjust to fit snugly.

③ Fill the pastry bag three-quarters full with filling or icing.

④ Use a bench scraper on the outside of the bag to push the icing towards the tip.

⑤ Twist together the top of the pastry bag and hold with your hand to ensure the icing stays in the bag while you're piping.

Filling a Cake with Icing

Adding icing to cake layers is one of my favorite processes because of how animating it can be: This is when you can invent unusual flavor and color combinations and see your cake start to take form. I've always found it helpful to pipe the filling onto the cake layer in order to get an even amount on each layer, but you could also spread the icing on with a flat spatula.

TOOLS:

• cake turntable
• filled pastry bag with
  medium round piping tip (#04)
• large flat spatula

❶ Pipe a circle of icing around the outer edge of a cake layer as a starting guide.

❷ Starting at the center of the cake layer, pipe an even amount of filling, spiraling until you reach the outer edge of icing.

❸ With a large flat spatula, even out the filling. Repeat with each cake layer, leaving the top cake bare. (If you're making an open layered cake, see page 191; you'll need to ice the top layer as well for a finished look.) Refrigerate the iced cake layers for about 10 minutes before stacking for easier assembly.

Stacking Cake Layers

Once you've iced all your cake layers, it's time to stack them to make a completed cake or tier. For an open layered cake (without icing on the sides, like the cake pictured on page 190), this would be the final step of icing before inserting dowels for a tiered cake.

TOOLS:

• scissors

❶ After chilling the iced cake layers for about 10 minutes, remove them from the refrigerator. Using your hand as a guide, carefully slide one cake layer off its cake board and onto the base layer below. Repeat if adding more layers.

❷ Place the last, un-iced layer (or the final iced layer, if you are making an open layered cake) on the very top. For tiered cakes, use scissors to trim away excess cake board around the base, then place the cake and cake board atop a larger cake board for handling.

Crumb-Coating a Cake

After stacking your cake layers, it's helpful to apply what's called a *crumb coat* of icing to the cake to prevent any crumbs from getting into the final icing coat and to create an even surface. For a roughly iced cake effect, this would be the final step of icing before inserting dowels for a tiered cake.

TOOLS:
- cake turntable
- large flat spatula
- bench scraper

❶ Place a dollop of icing on top of the stacked cake.

❷ Using a flat spatula, spread the icing on the top and over the edge of the cake.

❸ Continue spreading icing on the side of the cake, keeping the icing as smooth as possible. Only use enough icing to lightly cover the cake; it should appear transparent.

❹ Go over the side of the cake with a bench scraper to achieve a smoother surface, removing excess icing if necessary.

❺ With the flat spatula, smooth from the edge into the center of the cake to create even corners and a smooth top surface, holding the spatula above the cake and then bringing it down to the edge of the cake in a swooping motion to smooth the edge. Refrigerate for about an hour before applying your final coat of icing.

Adding the Final Icing Coat

In order to achieve a smooth icing coat, it's helpful to use room temperature icing, and re-beat it to restore the texture if it's been refrigerated. Keeping your spatula and bench scraper clean throughout the different steps will also help. If you are covering a cake with fondant, you'll want to ice it first, so the cake layers don't show through and the fondant lies smoothly and evenly over the cake.

TOOLS:

• cake turntable
• large flat spatula
• bench scraper

❶ Place a large dollop of icing on top of a crumb-coated cake.

❷ With a large flat spatula, smooth the icing on top of the cake just until it peeks over the edge.

❸ Smooth the icing around the edge to create a small ledge around the top. This will help achieve distinct, angled corners when doing final touches.

❹ Spread the icing on the side of the cake until completely covered. The goal is to keep the icing as smooth and even as possible.

❺ With a bench scraper, go lightly around the side of the cake to make an even coat. This may take a few tries.

❻ Using the spatula and the same swooping motion as on page 113, bring the extra icing on the corners toward the center of the cake, smoothing and evening out the top. Repeat until the edge and top are completely even and smooth. Refrigerate the finished cake for at least 1 hour before stacking the tiers and decorating.

Covering a Cake with Fondant

Use powdered sugar instead of cornstarch when you're rolling out fondant so that it won't dry out as quickly. Work on a clean wood or nonstick surface. Start with a final smooth-coated cake (see page 114) that has been chilled for at least an hour.

For cakes that have sharp edges, such as the square and hexagonal cakes on pages 243 and 257, you can use the technique shown below, or you can also apply the fondant in panels to each surface to emphasize the shapes. To apply fondant panels to a shape, measure all surfaces and make mockups on parchment paper. Roll fondant out thinly and trim the shapes carefully with a utility knife. Apply the fondant shapes first to the sides of the cakes and then to the top, covering the icing. The fondant will stick to the smooth icing. Use a cake smoother to make sure all sides are flat.

TOOLS:

- nonstick work surface
- powdered sugar
  (in a muslin bag for dusting)
- silicone rolling pin
- cake smoother
- pastry cutter or small knife
- sewing pin
- utility knife

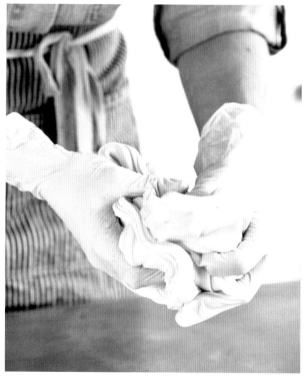

❶ Knead the fondant on a nonstick surface to bring it to room temperature. Tap the muslin bag on your work surface to dust it with powdered sugar.

❷ Using a silicone rolling pin, roll out the fondant to a ⅛-inch to ¹⁄₁₆-inch thickness. Rotate evenly as you roll out the fondant as you would for a piecrust. If the fondant begins to stick, dust more powdered sugar on the surface.

❸ Keep your hands dusted with powdered sugar to prevent sticking. Gently slide your hands underneath the piece of fondant, palms up.

❹ Place the fondant over the chilled, iced cake.

❺ Working from the top of the cake down, use a cake smoother and your hands to smooth out the very top of the cake to the corners and then smooth the side. I find it helpful to stretch out the edge of the fondant as I'm smoothing the side.

❻ Trim off excess fondant around the edge with a pastry cutter or small knife, leaving 1 inch of fondant around the base.

❼ Press the fondant in lightly to create a good seal around the base of the cake.

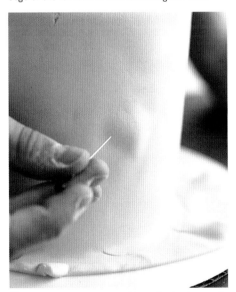

❽ If any air bubbles are visible in the fondant, poke them diagonally with a sewing pin and then smooth out with the cake smoother.

❾ With a utility knife, trim off all excess fondant so it is flush with the base.

❿ Peel away the excess fondant. Keep the cake well refrigerated, for a least 1 hour or overnight, until you're ready to stack the tiers and decorate the cake.

Using Straws to Support Cake Tiers

Keeping the weight of your cake evenly balanced is critical to successfully stacking cake tiers. Placing sturdy jumbo straws, available at cake-decorating stores, in between the cake boards and a dowel down the center of an entire tiered cake allows the weight to be distributed evenly, which will enable your tiered cake to stand tall for traveling or being on display for a long period of time. Tiered cakes can be made with open layered cakes, iced cakes, or fondant-covered cakes. It is important that the cake and icing are even so that when the straws are placed, they will be even as well, for an evenly balanced, stable tiered cake. Insert the straws into each tier before you stack them (see page 122).

TOOLS:

• cake boards

• sturdy jumbo straws

• scissors

❶ Place a cake board that is 2 inches smaller than the cake on top of a chilled cake, in the center, as a guide. Use a straw to make 4 to 8 marks evenly in the icing around the cake board. Remove the cake board. Larger cakes will need more straws to support the weight. For a starting reference: Use 4 straws for a 4-inch cake and 8 straws for a 12-inch cake.

❷ Following the marks, insert the straws vertically into the cake so that they go through the entire cake. It is important to keep the straws as straight as possible.

❸ Trim each straw with scissors so that it is flush with the top of the cake.

❹ Press each straw in to ensure it is inserted fully and flush with the cake.

❺ Repeat with all tiers except the top tier, keeping the other cakes refrigerated while you work.

Stacking Cake Tiers

When stacking cake tiers, have handy a piping bag with a small round tip, filled with the cake's icing (for an iced cake) or royal icing (for a fondant-covered cake) to act as glue in between the cake tiers and for covering up the hole on the top tier created by the wooden dowel.

TOOLS:
- piping bag with a small round tip filled with icing or royal icing
- large flat spatula
- wooden dowel
- pencil-sharpener or utility knife
- clippers or small handsaw

❶ Start with the bottom tier, most likely the largest cake. Pipe a small amount of icing on top of each straw as well as in the very center of the cake.

❷ Take out the cake that will be tiered next, most likely one size smaller. Place a large flat spatula under the cake board and lift the cake up.

❸ Center the cake on top of the previous tier, leaving the cake board underneath the cake for support. Continue stacking the cakes on top of one another until you reach the top tier.

❹ Place a dowel next to the cake and mark the height of the cake on the dowel with a pencil.

❺ Trim the dowel with the clippers or a small handsaw. Shave down the rough end to a point (I find using an electric pencil sharpener most helpful, but a utility knife works as well).

❻ Insert the sharpened dowel through the center of the cake until it reaches the bottom. The dowel is essential for keeping the layers aligned in a tiered cake. If measured correctly, the dowel should not be sticking out of the icing.

❼ Pipe a small amount of icing where the dowel went through the top of the cake and smooth it over with spatula.

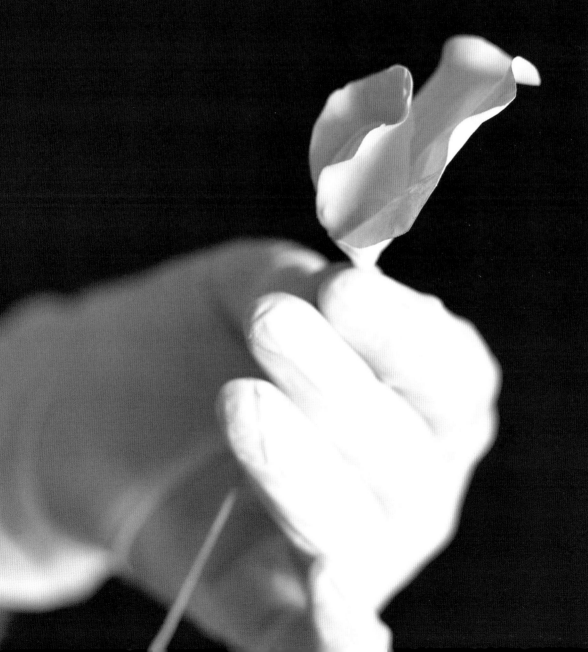

~⌒~ ⑤ ~⌒~

working with fondant,
sugar paste, and marzipan

When it comes to how each of these sugar doughs is worked, fondant, sugar paste, and marzipan are similar in many ways, although they do have some differences. Each is better for certain uses, depending on what you want for the finished product.

For example, fondant stays soft after it is shaped, making it suitable for covering cakes and applying two-dimensional decorations; sugar paste becomes hard and brittle once it dries, so it can hold a three-dimensional shape but should not be used to cover a cake. Sugar paste is most commonly used to create flowers, leaves, and any other decoration or shape that needs extra structure during sculpting. The added stability also provides longevity for decorating and storing. For instance, when ruffling the edge of a flower petal, sugar paste will hold the ruffle, while fondant would not. Tutorials on making various kinds of sugar paste flowers and leaves begin on page 137.

Marzipan has a grainy texture from the ground almonds. You can sculpt it like clay, but it isn't the best for rolling out like fondant, or for making delicate shapes like sugar paste. It's ideal for sculpting items such as fruits, which aren't naturally super smooth, such as the peaches on page 169.

Fondant, sugar paste, and marzipan all act as a magnet for the smallest pieces of dust, whether from your hands, work surface, tools, or apron. So before you start working, clean all surfaces, including your rolling pin and any other tools, wear a clean apron, wash your hands or wear gloves, and use a nonporous nonstick surface (such as a large cutting mat or your countertop) and plastic or silicone rolling pin.

To roll out fondant or sugar paste, first knead it on a nonstick surface until it becomes malleable. Lightly dust your surface with powdered sugar (for fondant) or cornstarch (for sugar paste), then, using a plastic or silicone rolling pin, roll out the fondant or sugar paste like a piecrust, rotating it as necessary and making sure to keep the shape and thickness even. Generally I roll fondant for covering a cake to a thickness of $\frac{1}{8}$ inch, and sugar paste for flowers and leaves very thinly, to about $\frac{1}{16}$ inch.

A multitude of cutters is available to make specific shapes from thinly rolled-out sugar paste, including leaves, flowers, shapes, letters, and numbers. Silicone molds can be used to transfer realistic textures onto sugar paste cutouts (such as veins on leaves, as on the Sweet Peas and Ferns cake on page 195), or to mold it into shapes (such as the Brooch Flowers cake on page 232). Sugar paste can also be rolled out and cut by hand to make custom shapes and designs, such as feathers (page 218) and flags (page 244).

To keep fondant or sugar paste from drying out, cover with a damp tea towel that has been wrapped in plastic wrap while working. If the fondant or sugar paste seems hard to work with or is cracking, it most likely is drying out. To bring it back to a workable material, knead a small amount of corn syrup or vegetable glycerin into it on a nonstick surface brushed with palm oil shortening. Knead the dough until all the ingredients are incorporated and it has a smooth, pliable texture.

The texture of the fondant or sugar paste often reflects the temperature of the environment and sometimes even the temperature of your hands. If it is sticking to your surface, hands, or rolling pin, lightly dust the work surface: Use powdered sugar for fondant (cornstarch would dry it out), and cornstarch for sugar paste (powdered sugar can add too much moisture and keep the decorations from drying properly).

Wrapping a Tea Towel in Plastic Wrap

Sugar paste and fondant both dry out quickly when left uncovered. I came up with this easy solution to keep your fondant and sugar paste pieces in an ideal condition while you're working. You'll find me using this great trick throughout the tutorials in the cake chapters.

TOOLS:

- plastic wrap
- damp tea towel folded in half

❶ On a flat surface, pull a piece of plastic wrap the length of the folded towel (don't cut it yet).

❷ Neatly place the damp tea towel on the plastic wrap. Make sure all creases are smoothed out of the tea towel.

❸ Cut the plastic wrap so it is long enough to fold over the tea towel.

❹ Fold all sides of the plastic wrap tightly over the tea towel to cover it, smoothing out any creases in the plastic.

❺ When working with fondant or sugar paste, set it on the smooth side of the plastic-wrapped tea towel (the side without the overlapping edges of the plastic wrap) and fold the towel over the fondant or sugar paste to prevent it from drying out.

Storing

After a cake is covered or decorated with fondant, it will keep at room temperature, uncovered, for 4 to 5 hours. If you are refrigerating it (for no longer than 2 days for the freshest results), the cake needs to be stored in a cardboard box because the moisture in a refrigerator will cause the fondant to sweat and eventually melt. For extra protection, wrap the box in plastic wrap, which will further help keep moisture from reaching the cake. Some refrigerators are now built with humidity controls, but if you're not sure, it's better to take the extra precaution.

Allow sugar paste decorations to dry out completely in a cool, dry environment. Most decorations take 48 hours to 1 week to fully dry. You'll find that when sugar paste dries out, it becomes very brittle. It is also highly sensitive to its environment and will wilt in moisture, including humidity.

Let marzipan sculptures dry for at least 1 to 2 days before using or storing.

Once completely dried, keep sugar paste and marzipan decorations in an airtight container lined with egg crate foam. The foam not only acts as a cushion for the delicate decorations, but also will draw out any moisture. If kept in an airtight container in a cool, dry environment, sugar paste and marzipan decorations will last up to 6 months to 1 year.

Adding Color

If a specific hue of fondant, sugar paste, or marzipan is desired, you can add all-natural food coloring. I often wear gloves when adding dye to keep my hands color free! Add a couple drops of liquid food coloring at a time to a small amount of fondant, sugar paste, or marzipan and knead on a nonstick surface until there are no longer any streaks. To achieve a stronger hue, add more dye in small increments. Because fondant, sugar paste, and marzipan are slightly different colors to begin with, the finished colors may be different from one to another. Natural powder dyes can be used as well, but will result in more subtle, earthy tones, usually with speckles throughout.

You can also paint sugar and marzipan decorations with either dry or wet dyes after they have dried. This is one of the most enjoyable and rewarding experiences of cake decorating, as the minute details really come to life when you had a hint of extra color here and there. You'll be amazed! For flowers and leaves, I often apply a dry dusting of powder dye with a paintbrush on the edges and areas where highlights or shadows are desired. Use a darker hue for shadows and a lighter hue for highlights. While dry dusting results in a subtle finish, wet painting gives a bolder, more deliberate look. Turn to page 233 to see examples of both dry dusting and wet painting on sugar brooches.

Making Sugar Paste Flowers and Leaves

Sugar flowers and leaves arranged artfully on a cake can create a unique design. Sculpting sugar flowers and leaves to look as though they're genuine is an effortful achievement that will show in the final product. The following techniques can be used as simple guides to create an array of various blossoms, flowers, and leaves. Using different shaped cutters and molds with the same instructions can result in drastically different creations.

Sculpting "Mexican Hat" Blossoms

Little sugar paste blossoms can be a great way to add a simple accent to a cake or to fill in any empty spots when arranging larger sugar flowers and leaves. A variety of small blossom cutters can be used with this technique to make different shapes.

USE THIS TECHNIQUE TO MAKE:

- Peach blossoms, Peachy Keen cake, page 169

TOOLS:

- small stamens
- 29-gauge wire, trimmed to 4-inch lengths
- green and white floral tape
- Sugar Paste (page 59)
- cornstarch in muslin bag for dusting
- silicone modeling tool
- blossom cutter
- ball tool
- 1:1 mixture of water and corn syrup
- cake dummy
- paintbrush
- green powder dye

❶ For each blossom, tightly secure 5 small stamens to the top of a wire with white floral tape.

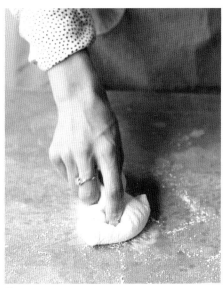

❷ Create a rounded cone shape from a small piece of sugar paste.

❸ Flatten the edges to resemble a hat.

❹ Dust a nonstick surface with cornstarch.

❺ Use a small silicone shaping tool to thin out the edges of the cone, rotating the cone evenly as you work.

❻ Use a blossom cutter to cut the edges of the cone into a flower shape, keeping the tapered cone in the center of the cutter.

❼ Remove the excess sugar paste with your fingers.

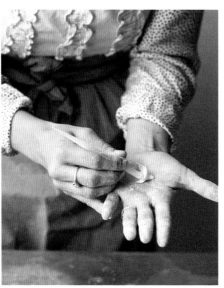

❽ Guide the blossom out of the cutter by pushing it gently with the round side of the shaping tool.

❾ Dust your hands with cornstarch. Holding the blossom in the palm of your hand, shape the petals using a small ball tool so that they are rounded and thin.

❿ Dip the stamen wire into the water–corn syrup mixture.

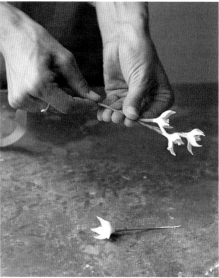

⓫ Insert the stamen wire through the center of the blossom, guiding the flower to the end of the stamens where the white floral tape begins.

⓬ Taper the bottom of the blossom, taking off any excess sugar paste. Insert the wire into a cake dummy and let the blossom dry for 48 hours to 1 week before continuing with the next step.

⓭ Once the blossoms are dry, wrap green floral tape around the tapered ends of blossoms. To assemble multiple blossoms, stagger them in bunches and wrap them with green floral tape.

14 Using a paintbrush and green powder dye, dry-dust the underside of the blossoms.

Sculpting Flowers on Wire

This technique is used to create a flower with petals that lay directly around the center and that can be layered with more petals to create a fuller look. Sizes vary from small flowers, such as these daisies, to larger flowers, such as roses.

USE THIS TECHNIQUE TO MAKE:

- Sweet peas, Sweet Peas and Ferns cake, page 195
- Ranunculus, Posies cake, page 209
- Thistles, Gold in Chaos cake, page 290
- Abstract flowers, Mod Earth cake, page 293
- Daisies, Vintage Tin cake, page 309

TOOLS:

- Sugar Paste (page 59)
- 20-gauge wire, trimmed to 8-inch lengths
- 1:1 mixture of water and corn syrup
- flower center mold
- cornstarch in muslin bag for dusting
- cake dummy
- silicone rolling pin
- daisy cutter
- damp tea towel wrapped in plastic wrap (see page 134)
- foam pad
- small-medium ball tool
- paintbrushes
- green floral tape
- green powder dye

❶ For each flower, to make the center, roll a small amount of sugar paste (here, yellow) into a smooth ball.

❷ Taper one side of the flower center into a cone shape.

❸ Bend one end of the wire into a hook shape to better secure it to the sugar paste. Dip the hooked end into the water–corn syrup mixture. Insert the hooked end of the wire into the tapered end of the sugar paste ball.

❹ Further taper the end of the cone around the wire, removing excess sugar paste.

❺ Flatten the rounded top of the flower center.

❻ Dust a flower center mold with cornstarch.

❼ Gently press the sugar paste center onto the mold to make an impression.

❽ With your fingers, soften and smooth out the edges of the flower center. Insert the center into a cake dummy and let dry for 48 hours to 1 week before continuing with the next step.

❾ To make the petals, roll out sugar paste (here, white) on a cornstarch-dusted nonstick surface to a thickness of $1/16$ inch.

⑩ Use a flower cutter, such as a daisy, to cut out flowers. Smooth off any rough edges with your fingers.

⑪ Place the sugar paste flowers in a plastic-wrapped tea towel and cover them while you work.

⑫ Working with one flower at a time, place the flower on a cornstarch-dusted foam pad. Use a small-medium ball tool to round, shape, and thin the petals.

⑬ Use the ball tool to gently curl a few petals inward.

14 With a paintbrush, wet the bottom of the flower center with the water–corn syrup mixture.

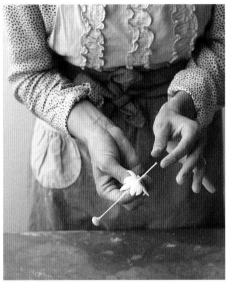

15 Insert the flower center through the shaped petals.

16 Press the underside gently to adhere the petals to the center. Insert the flowers into a cake dummy, then bend the wires so that the flowers are drying upside down so the petals keep their rounded shape while drying. Let dry for 48 hours to 1 week before continuing with the next steps.

17 Once the flowers are dry, wrap green floral tape around the wires, starting from the underside of the flower and ending at the bottom of the wire.

18 To finish each flower, use a dry paintbrush and green powder dye to dry-dust the underside of the flower.

Sculpting Petals on Wire

Sculpting petals individually on wires is best when making larger flowers that need movement.

USE THIS TECHNIQUE TO MAKE:

- Hellebores, Iridescent Black cake, page 228
- Bayahibe rose, Dripping Pearls cake, page 237
- Orchids, A White Cake, page 299
- Double tulips, peony, and mini poppies, Vintage Tin cake, page 309

TOOLS:

- cornstarch in a muslin bag for dusting
- silicone rolling pin
- Sugar Paste (page 59)
- petal cutters
- damp tea towel wrapped in plastic wrap (see page 134)
- foam pad
- large and small-medium ball tools
- silicone veining mold
- 24-gauge wire, trimmed to 6-inch lengths
- 1:1 mixture of water and corn syrup
- fruit carton
- white and green floral tape
- medium-size stamens
- powder dyes
- vodka
- paintbrushes

❶ On a cornstarch-dusted nonstick surface, roll out the sugar paste, rotating evenly, to a thickness of ¹/₁₆ inch. Cut out various sized petal shapes using petal cutters, setting the petals on a plastic-wrapped tea towel and covering them while you work.

❷ Working with one petal at a time, place the petal on a cornstarch-dusted foam pad, and use a large ball tool to thin out the petal.

❸ Place the thinned petal on a cornstarch-dusted silicone veining mold and press gently to make an impression. Gently remove from the mold. Place the veined petal back on the foam pad and use a small-medium ball tool to ruffle the edges.

❹ Dip the end of a wire into the water–corn syrup mixture. Place the wet wire onto the end of the petal.

❺ Pinch the underside of the petal to adhere the sugar paste to the wire.

❻ Set the finished petals in a fruit carton and let dry for 48 hours to 1 week before continuing with the next step.

❼ To make the flower center, use white floral tape to secure a bunch of medium-size stamens to a wire. Mix yellow powder dye with vodka and use a paintbrush to paint the stamens.

❽ Once the petals have dried, attach them to the center one at a time, starting with the smallest petals and ending with the largest, wrapping green floral tape around the wires. A small flower will take 5 to 8 petals, while a larger flower will take 12 to 15 petals.

❾ Once all the petals have been attached, wrap the entire wire with green floral tape.

10 To finish the flower, use a paintbrush and powder dye to dry-dust the petals, creating shadows and highlights on the ruffles and veins.

Sculpting Leaves on Wire

Sugar leaves can be a wonderful accent to a cake, either in combination with flowers or on their own. Sculpting leaves on wires will give you the flexibility to create movement, whether attaching them to flower stems or grouping the leaves together with floral tape. As with flowers, any size or shape leaf cutter can be used with this technique.

USE THIS TECHNIQUE FOR:

- Sugar Eucalyptus cake, page 183
- Mod Earth cake, page 293
- Vintage Tin cake, page 309
- Gold in Chaos cake, page 290

TOOLS:

- cornstarch in a muslin bag for dusting
- silicone rolling pin
- Sugar Paste (page 59)
- leaf cutter
- damp tea towel wrapped in plastic wrap (see page 134)
- foam pad
- medium ball tool
- silicone vein mold
- 24-gauge green wire, trimmed to 6-inch lengths
- 1:1 mixture of water and corn syrup
- fruit carton
- green floral tape
- paintbrush
- powder dye

❶ On a cornstarch-dusted nonstick surface, roll out the sugar paste, rotating evenly, to a thickness of 1/16 inch. Using the leaf cutter, cut out multiple leaves from the rolled-out sugar paste.

❷ Place the sugar paste leaves onto the plastic wrapped tea towel and cover while you work.

❸ Working with one at a time, place a leaf on a cornstarch-dusted foam pad, and use a medium ball tool to thin out the leaf.

❹ Place the thinned-out leaf on a cornstarch-dusted silicone vein mold and press gently to make an impression. Gently remove from the mold.

❺ Dip the end of a green wire into the water–corn syrup mixture.

6 Place the wet end of the wire on the end of a sugar paste leaf.

7 Pinch the underside of the leaf to adhere the sugar paste to the wire.

8 Place the leaves on the fruit carton to shape and dry. Let dry for 48 hours to 1 week before handling or assembling.

9 Once the leaves are dry, assemble multiple leaves by staggering them in bunches and wrapping them with green floral tape.

⑩ To finish the leaves, dry-dust with a paintbrush and powder dye, creating shadows and highlights on the ruffles and veins.

aspects of
cake design

Top View:

Creating edible art is never mundane for me; it's one of the reasons I fell in love with being a chef.

Being able to *bring my imagination to life* on a daily basis, and have someone literally consume it, is unbelievably rewarding. Creating cake designs requires focus and precision, but also an eye for organic, harmonious composition. For each cake I create, I make a detailed sketch beforehand, which acts as a blueprint. However, I find that as they come to life, my ideas are usually transformed into something entirely new.

Throughout the sculpting and design demonstrations on the following pages you'll find a repeating theme that I encourage you to incorporate into your own practices: the balance of precision and ease, no matter what style of design.

When building your cake, it's important to follow the guidelines on the previous pages in order to understand the materials and their limitations. This allows room for your imagination when it comes to the creative direction of your designs. I embrace the idea of not following concrete rules in cake designs: Be your own art director in your sculpting and cake design. There are no right or wrong answers when it comes to the aesthetic of decorating. The following chapters should expand the way you think about cake and give you inspiration to create designs beyond your dreams. After all, it is cake—don't take it *too* seriously!

~ 6 ~

classical

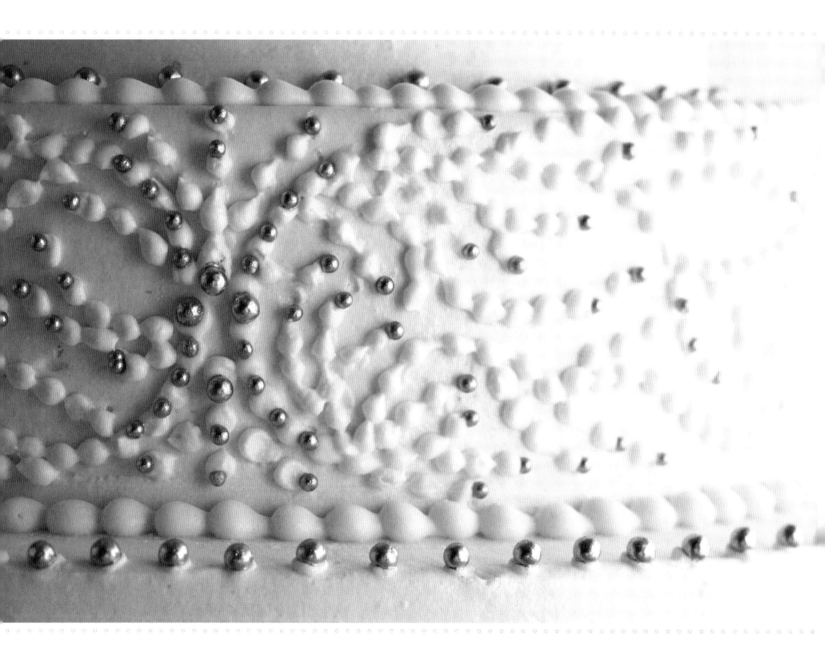

As much as I love inventive designs,
a classical aesthetic can be just as important.

I t's key to study fundamental techniques—such as different styles of icing, piping, arranging fresh and sugar flowers, and other simple decorations—before you press on to achieve more innovative designs. This natural progression will help you better grasp the more contemporary designs featured later, and you'll still find your personal style coming through with these classical methods.

The fundamentals in this chapter include using fresh flowers and fruit as well as sugar flowers and leaves; simple and intricate piping; brush embroidery; incorporating confections such as truffles as a decoration; and sculpting marzipan fruit. All of the cakes on the following pages are round, with proportional tier heights, and are iced simply, covered in fondant, or even left un-iced. Traditional colors are often soft and muted with occasional accents of gold.

I find it helpful to compile a list of all the techniques you'd like to learn and then check them off one at a time so you don't become too overwhelmed. Approach new methods with an open mind. And don't worry about making everything perfect: Imperfection and individuality will make your cakes stand out, and you'll have more fun in the process.

fresh blooms

THERE IS SOMETHING so graceful about a simply iced cake accented with garden fresh flowers. Keeping a design to the basics, without frills, showcases the simple shapes in the icing and the visual and aromatic experience of the blooms.

TO CREATE THE VERTICAL STRIPES IN THE ICING, apply a rough coat of icing to each tier. Drag a small spatula gently through the icing from the bottom of the tier to just above the top. Repeat just next to the first stripe so that the edge overlaps, then continue to make vertical stripes around the entire tier. To smooth out the top edge, sweep a large spatula towards you, starting above the cake, touching down at the edge of the cake, and then lifting off at the center. Scrape excess icing off the spatula as you work. Continue this motion until you've made your way around the entire tier. Refrigerate the tiers for about 30 minutes before stacking and decorating with flowers.

The most common ways to arrange flowers on a cake are randomly, centralized, or cascading. In this design I arranged the flowers randomly. Start by placing the larger flowers, inserting the floral tape-covered stem into the icing and cake, in small bunches around the cake. Continue to fill in with smaller flowers, and finish by placing thin-stemmed blooms gently peeking out from the bunches. This creates an organic, lush bouquet.

When using fresh flowers to decorate a cake, wrap the ends with floral tape to keep the stems from touching the inside of the cake and icing. Be aware that many flowers are inedible or have been grown using pesticides. If you have a local farmers' market or access to a fresh garden in the right seasons, a few of my favorite edible blooms are arugula, chamomile, chrysanthemums, honeysuckle, lavender, pansies, peas, roses, and violets. Here, I arranged flowers given to me by my florist friend, Liza Lubell: scabiosa, antique garden roses, privet, and gomphrena.

To protect flowers from wilting, keep the cake in a covered box in the refrigerator, or store in a dark, cool environment until it's time to display it. When on display, place the cake in a cool environment out of direct sunlight. Remove the flowers before slicing the cake. If using edible blooms, you can then use them as accents on each plate.

peachy keen

THIS CAKE SHOWCASES painted gold details along with sculpted marzipan peaches and sugar paste blossoms and leaves. I painted the ornate gold patterns using a stencil first and then embellished them freehand; you may use any color that fits your design. For this technique, I've found that mixing powder dyes with vodka works best because you can control the consistency of the liquid.

Fondant cakes usually work best for painting. If you are working on an iced cake, make sure your final coat of icing is smooth and the cake is chilled before painting. Commonly, cake stencils come in the width and height of a large cake tier. To avoid the obstacle of applying such a large stencil, and also to have a say in the design, I generally trim out my favorite parts of the stencil to use separately.

TO MAKE MARZIPAN PEACHES, knead orange liquid dye into Marzipan (page 63) to produce a subtle orange color. Roll the marzipan into uniform balls in various sizes from small to large, with the largest being the size of an actual peach. Gently shape them into peaches, allowing some fingerprints to stay on the surface for a natural texture. Use a skewer to poke a hole from the top center and another from the bottom. This will give each peach a natural concave shape at both ends, help it dry, and provide a place to insert the flowering branch. Create a crease from the top of the peach down the center using a boning tool or knife. Once the peaches have dried, dry-dust them using a paintbrush and powder dye in darker hues of orange and coral to create natural-looking coloration, then finish off with a light dusting of cornstarch.

TO MAKE THE PEACH BLOSSOMS, follow the Mexican Hat how-to on page 138. Group sprigs of blossoms and leaves (see page 152) and wrap them with brown floral tape to create stems for the peaches. Insert the end of the arrangement into the top hole of a marzipan peach until secure. Insert toothpicks into the bottom of the peaches to secure them on the cake.

Painting and Stenciling Adornments

When creating an ornate painted cake design, I'll often start with a stencil for a base and then complete the details by hand, painting around what I've begun with the stencil. I find this helps not only to create balance within the placement but also balance within the design elements. Using a mixture of stenciling and hand painting creates fluidity within a fixed design.

TOOLS:

- vodka
- FDA-certified edible gold dust
- stencils
- fine-tipped paintbrushes

❶ In a small bowl, stir vodka into the gold dust until any lumps dissipate and a paintable liquid forms. You may need to add more liquid throughout the process if your paint becomes too thick.

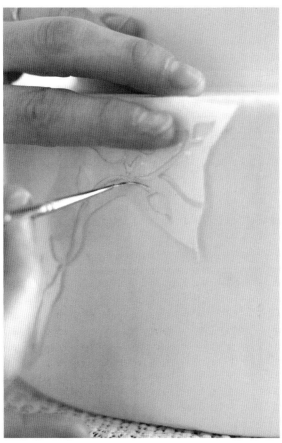

❷ Gently hold the stencil against the cake. With the small brush, outline the shapes in the stencil, making sure not to move the stencil as you're working.

❸ After you've painted stencil patterns where you desire, use the fine paintbrush to paint patterns and organic shapes freehand to fill in the spaces around the stenciled patterns. When painting freely, start off with simple lines and shapes. Then layer upon this until you're satisfied with the design. The paint will dry quickly.

icing domes

DEHYDRATED FRUITS AND VEGETABLES are a great alternative to artificial dyes and produce gorgeous natural colors. Dehydrated black mulberries and green tea powder are mixed into these icings to create subtle blue and green hues. To use dehydrated fruits and vegetables in icing, grind them into a fine powder using a food processor, then stir 1 tablespoon into the icing at a time until you reach the color you desire. Plants and vegetables that are bitter or strong in flavor, such as wheatgrass or turmeric, will alter the flavor of the icing, so it's best to avoid them.

TO PIPE DOMED ICING DOTS, use a pastry bag fitted with a large round tip. Hold the bag with the tip about ½ inch away from the surface of the cake. Apply pressure until the icing forms a dome, then release the pressure and pull the piping bag directly upward away from the dome. Here, I finished the dots by placing a blueberry on top of each dome.

chocolate drips

CHOCOLATE DRIPPING over cake tiers is very simple to produce and results in a festive, decadent cake design. A variety of icings pair well with ganache, including Rose Water–Raspberry Icing (page 67) and Espresso Icing (page 68); this tall tier features roughly spackled Strawberry-Basil Icing (page 67), which boasts flecks of fresh strawberry puree. Chocolate drips are a nice finish to a simple single tier or can be applied on a multi-tier cake.

Dripping Chocolate

Make sure your cake is chilled and the ganache is lukewarm so the icing on the cake doesn't melt when the chocolate is poured over.

TOOLS:
- Ganache (page 69)
- double boiler (or glass bowl and pot)
- ladle or small bowl
- large flat spatula

❶ Heat the ganache in a double boiler (I use a glass bowl over a pot of simmering water) until it is completely melted, then remove from the heat. Let cool, stirring every 5 minutes, until lukewarm, about 15 minutes. It should thicken up, but still have a flowing consistency. Pour a ladleful of ganache over the top of the chilled cake.

❷ Use the flat spatula to smooth the ganache slowly over the edge until you have your desired amount of drips. You can make the drips appear heavier or lighter depending on how much chocolate you allow to drip off. If you are making a tiered cake, apply the ganache to each tier separately and then refrigerate until firm before stacking.

adorned piping

THIS PIPING, TRADITIONAL IN STYLE, it is made more current by decorating only every other tier of the cake and piping in a more organic, almost sea-like pattern.

Piping an intricate design can take time, but try to enjoy the process. Always keep the cake well chilled as you apply the icing; if you find that your environment is warm, take a break and place the cake in the refrigerator for about half an hour. If you make a mistake or aren't happy with the design, a cold cake will make it easier to carefully and gently wipe off the piping with a flat spatula or bench scraper without affecting your smooth final coat. This cake's delicate design uses piped icing dots to create a pattern: Mark the design on the cake with a toothpick first for precision and then pipe on top of the toothpick marks using a pastry bag fitted with a very small round tip (#00). Embellish the design by applying gold dragées while the icing is soft; use tweezers for the most precise placement. For a more pristine look, the design can also be created with royal icing on a fondant-covered cake.

sugar eucalyptus

FONDANT COVERED TIERS create a clean, matte look, and the crisp lines of leaves and simple buds sculpted from sugar paste make a graceful accent. Dusting the green sprigs with a light blue powder dye not only creates depth and highlights, but also complements the light pink hue of the cake. When you want a tiered cake but don't need a large number of servings, stack small, shorter tiers to achieve a monumental presence even for a small gathering.

FOLLOW THE INSTRUCTIONS on page 152 to make long, slender eucalyptus leaves from green sugar paste, along with a few tiny buds from light-green sugar paste (you will need to let them dry for 48 hours to 1 week before arranging). Once dry, create small bouquets with the leaves and buds, securing them with green floral tape. Use a paintbrush and light blue powder dye to lightly dust the sprigs. Arrange the sprigs, inserting the wire into the icing and cake, sparsely around the edges of the tiers.

brush embroidery

ROYAL ICING is piped and then painted to resemble an organic stitched embroidery texture on this fondant covered cake.

After piping flower and leaf shapes using a very small round tip (#00), use a wet paintbrush to make strokes inwardly through the shapes. As much or as little detail can be added to create different looks using this method. You can create a motif using a stencil or freehand. For a natural flavor and hue, opt for unbleached, organic powdered sugar in your Royal Icing (page 64).

divine truffles

TRUFFLES, OF COURSE, are a delightful dessert on their own, but they can also be an unusually beautiful accent on a cake. The cake shown is Coconut Cake (page 85) with Espresso Icing (page 68), but truffles would also go well with a Mexican Chocolate Cake (page 73) with Lavender-Rosemary Icing (page 67) or Madagascar Vanilla Bean Cake (page 76) with Passion Fruit Icing (page 68).

Securing the truffles on the cake with toothpicks—inserting the toothpicks halfway into the truffles and then placing them into the cake—ensures that they stay in place and allows more options for placement within the design. Make sure to remove all toothpicks before serving to your guests!

Making Truffles

Truffles can be covered in a variety of ingredients, most commonly chopped nuts or cacao powder. Here I cover them with chopped pistachios.

TOOLS:

- Ganache (page 69)
- double boiler (or glass bowl and pot)
- rubber spatula
- canvas piping bag with a medium-size round piping tip (#04)
- parchment paper
- baking sheet
- chocolate
- rubber gloves
- chopped nuts or cacao powder for coating

❶ Heat the ganache in a double boiler (I use a glass bowl over a pot of simmering water), stirring with a rubber spatula, until melted. Let cool to room temperature, then place the ganache in the piping bag.

❷ On a parchment-lined baking sheet, pipe dollops of ganache in even lines, leaving about ½ inch between each dollop. Refrigerate for about 1 hour.

❸ Melt 2½ to 3 cups (about 500 grams) chopped chocolate in a double boiler; set aside. Fill a wide bowl or cake pan with chopped nuts (or cacao powder, if using).

❹ Wearing rubber gloves and working quickly, roll one dollop of ganache into a ball.

❺ Holding the ganache ball in one hand, dip the fingers of your other hand into the melted chocolate and roll them over the ball to lightly coat.

❻ After the ganache ball is lightly coated in chocolate, drop it into the chopped nut mixture or cocoa powder and cover completely.

❼ Repeat until all the ganache balls are covered. Refrigerate for 30 minutes before securing to the cake. Store truffles refrigerated in an airtight container.

naked layers

THIS DESIGN EXPOSES a cake's bare essentials. It highlights the most scrumptious part—the ingredients!

To make it, fill and stack the cake layers as described on pages 108 to 110, icing the top of each tier. For something unexpected, you could also layer different icings and cakes together for a multicolored flavor fusion.

Incorporating fresh fruit and herbs into a cake design creates a fresh, fun look. Make sure to lightly wash the fruit before using, and use toothpicks or thin skewers to hold the fruit in place.

Although this cake is shown with fruits and herbs, you can also decorate an open layered cake with other items including fresh flowers, sugar flowers, and marzipan confections. Modern decorations such as mushrooms (page 224) or sugar fans (page 227) could be used as well. Keep in mind that with no icing on the sides of the cake, you'll have less surface area to adhere designs to, so I recommend placing them around the base of the tiers.

sweet peas and ferns

QUAINT POLKA DOTS combined with realistic sugar sweet peas and ferns produce a nostalgically enchanting beauty. This cake is finished with Passion Fruit Icing (page 68) and dots of Madagascar Vanilla Bean Icing (page 66) piped with a small round tip (#01). After the dots are piped, you can lightly go over the peaks with a damp paintbrush to round the tops.

TO MAKE THE SUGAR SWEET PEAS, follow the general instructions for sculpting flowers on a wire on page 142, surrounding an oblong yellow flower center with two ruffled pink petals. Dry-dust the finished sweet peas with pink and yellow powder dye.

Sculpting Ferns on Wires

When attempting to sculpt replications from wildlife, seek imperfection and unevenness. Organisms in nature are not alike.

TOOLS:

- green Sugar Paste (page 59)
- cornstarch in a muslin bag for dusting
- large silicone rolling pin
- damp tea towel wrapped in plastic wrap (see page 134)
- fern cutter
- silicone fern imprint
- foam pad
- small-medium ball tool
- 24-gauge wire trimmed to 6-inch lengths
- 1:1 mixture of water and corn syrup
- fruit carton
- paintbrush
- green powder dye

❶ Knead the green sugar paste on a cornstarch-dusted nonstick surface to bring it to room temperature.

❷ Using the large silicone rolling pin, roll out the sugar paste to a thickness of ¹/₁₆ inch. Rotate the paste evenly, as you would for a piecrust. If the sugar paste begins to stick, dust more cornstarch on the surface. Cover any sugar paste that you are not using with the plastic-wrapped tea towel to prevent it from drying out.

❸ Use the fern-shaped cutter to cut out at least 10 fern shapes from the sugar paste. Place them inside the tea towel to prevent them from drying out.

❹ Working with one at a time, place each cutout on a silicone fern imprint. Press with even pressure to imprint the entire leaf. Gently remove the leaf.

❺ Place the leaf on a cornstarch-dusted foam pad. Use the ball tool to thin out the edges, rolling the ball tool in small back-and-forth motions to create rough, ruffled edges.

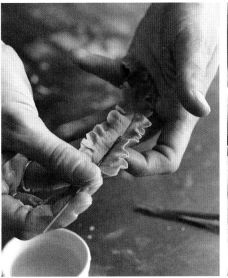

❻ Dip the end of a wire in a modest amount of the water–corn syrup mixture. Press the damp end of the wire in the center of the fern leaf, extending about one-quarter of the length of the leaf. Lightly pinch the sugar leaf onto the wire so that the wire does not show.

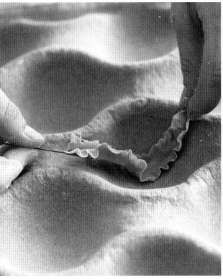

❼ Place in the fruit carton in a natural shape and let dry for at least 48 hours. To finish, dry-dust the leaf using the paintbrush with a darker shade of green powder. Dried spinach or kale powder works great for this.

7

classical
whimsy

In each of the following cakes, I combine an
unconventional design aspect with classic techniques
to create something bold.

W hen a whimsical touch is incorporated into a cake, the creation tends
to take on more of a playful look while still featuring classic techniques.
My goal is to have people forget that they're looking at cake and sugar
sculpture for a moment and be swept away into the design.

raveled bows

THE WAY FABRIC LAYS NATURALLY, even when it's manually tied into bows, can be incredibly graceful. This cake is my attempt to re-create this effect in sugar, with thinly rolled and cut fondant and sugar paste ribbons applied in the same manner as a ballerina's pointe shoes are laced.

The cake shown is covered with a smooth coat of icing, but the same technique could also be used on a fondant-covered cake. When working with iced cakes, it is important that they are well refrigerated before the decorations are applied.

TO RE-CREATE THIS DESIGN, cut ribbons in a few varying widths out of thinly rolled fondant, then trim each ribbon to the length of the cake's circumference (depending on how big a piece of fondant you roll initially, you may need to piece together multiple ribbons to encircle the cake). Use a paintbrush to lightly dab each ribbon's end with a mixture of equal parts water and corn syrup and fold the corners inwards to make tapered ends; this is where the bows will be placed. Press the fondant lightly to the icing to adhere all around the tiers, crisscrossing ribbons of different widths to allow the ends to meet at different points.

The bows and tails are made from sugar paste in order to give the shapes more body and make them appear draped without breaking. As you make the bows and tails, apply them to the cake right away (without letting them dry first) so that they fall naturally. Place the bows where each pair of tapered ribbon ends meet; the cake here has bows not only at the front of the cake, but also around the sides and back as well. This creates depth within the layers.

TO MAKE THE BOWS AND RIBBON TAILS, thinly roll out sugar paste and cut out strips in the same varying widths as the ribbons. For each bow, make a loop with the sugar paste strip and glue the ends in the center with corn syrup–water mixture, then lightly pinch the center. Wrap another piece of the same width around the center of the loop, affix it with corn syrup mixture, and trim the ends. For the tails, cut a sugar paste strip crosswise into two uneven pieces and trim the ends as desired. On the cake shown, they are cut in different styles, some on the diagonal and some with forked ends. Taper the untrimmed edges as you did for the fondant ribbons. First adhere the tapered edge of the tails onto the tapered ends of the ribbons, and then attach the bow on top of the tails, using corn syrup–water mixture as glue and matching each set of bow and tails to a ribbon of the same width. Alternate applying the bows and tails around the cake so that they can overlap one another.

posies

THE COMBINATION of two-dimensional and three-dimensional decorations in this cake excites the senses in an imaginative way: It not only keeps your eyes leaping around the design, but also in and out of different visual fields. Creating the two-dimensional blossoms in sugar paste rather than painting them directly on the cake intensifies this experience.

TO MAKE THE FLAT PIECES, use blossom and leaf cutters to cut shapes from rolled-out sugar paste, then let dry for 48 hours. Mix powder dye and vodka to make a liquid and use a fine-tip paintbrush to paint on the details. If applying to an iced cake, such as the one shown, the pieces will adhere directly to the icing; if applying them to a fondant-covered cake, use a small dot of royal icing to help them stay in place. The two-dimensional pieces should appear flat, not flush with the cake.

FOR THE THREE-DIMENSIONAL SUGAR FLOWERS, in addition to the ranunculus blossoms (instructions follow), follow the instructions on page 152 to create sugar paste leaves on wire. Ranunculus leaves tend to have accentuated rough, ruffled edges. Make a few small yellow centers to accent the arrangements, following the steps on page 142 for creating centers for blossoms.

Sculpting Ranunculus

When sculpting a flower that has a large bulb center, it's helpful to use a Styrofoam ball for a base, which not only saves time but also keeps the weight much lighter and the flower easier to work with while decorating a cake. Ranunculus can either be tight and round or open and ruffled—the type of flowers you want will affect the way you shape the petals. Whenever you're sculpting with sugar, you should familiarize yourself with the interior and exterior anatomy of the subject—in this case, ranunculus—to help achieve a natural look. I often become more aware of the natural gesture when I'm sculpting from an actual flower.

TOOLS:

- pliers
- 20-gauge wire trimmed to 7-inch lengths
- Royal Icing (page 64)
- at least 10 small Styrofoam balls
- yellow and red Sugar Paste (page 59)
- silicone flower center mold or cone-shaped veining tool
- 1:1 mixture of water and corn syrup
- Styrofoam cake dummy (for drying finished flowers)
- cornstarch in a muslin bag for dusting
- large silicone rolling pin
- damp tea towel wrapped in plastic wrap (see page 134)
- small circle cutter
- foam board
- small-medium ball tool
- paintbrush

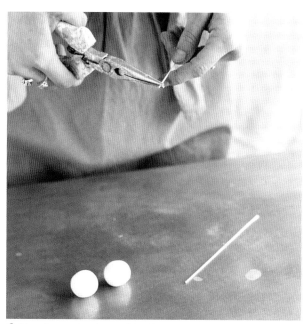

❶ Use pliers to bend a small hook at the end of each wire. This will help keep the wire in place throughout the process of making the ranunculus.

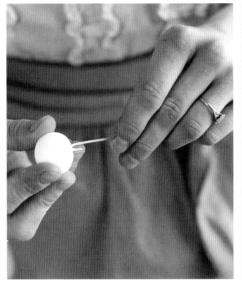

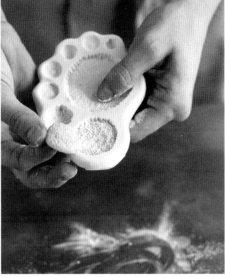

❷ Dip the bent end of the wire into royal icing and then insert it into a Styrofoam ball.

❸ Press a pea-size amount of yellow sugar paste in a flower center mold to make a realistic impression. If you don't have a flower center mold, use the pointed end of a cone-shaped veining tool to make marks that resemble a flower center.

❹ Use the water–corn syrup mixture to glue the sugar center on top of the Styrofoam ball. Set aside in the cake dummy to dry. Make at least 10 centers.

❺ Dust your surface with cornstarch. Using the silicone rolling pin, roll out the red sugar paste to a thickness of $1/16$ inch. Rotate the paste evenly as you roll, as you would for a piecrust. If the sugar paste begins to stick, dust more cornstarch on the surface. Cover with the plastic-wrapped tea towel to prevent the sugar paste from drying out.

6 Using the small circle cutter, cut out 50 to 70 circles from the sugar paste for the ranunculus petals, covering them with the tea towel as you work to prevent the sugar paste from drying out. You will need more petals—each flower with three rows of petals will require 24 to 30 petals total— but start by cutting out only the petals for the first row, then roll out more petals as you need them, so your sugar paste stays fresh as you work. This will also allow time for the petals to dry a bit before adding the next row.

7 Working with 5 to 7 at a time (the first row for each flower), place the sugar paste petals on a cornstarch-dusted foam board. Use the ball tool, gently working in circular motions, to thin out the sugar paste while creating a cup shape.

8 When the first row of sugar paste petals are thinned and shaped, brush a small amount of the water–corn syrup mixture on the inside of each petal.

9 Place the petals around the bud center, overlapping each one to create the first row. Roll out and cut more petals as needed, and repeat these steps to make more rows of petals, increasing the number of petals by 3 for each row. The more rows of petals you add, the fuller the flower will be: For a tight bulb as shown on the cake, I recommend applying 3 to 4 rows of sugar petals. For a full, open ranunculus, I recommend applying at least 10 to 12 rows. Either way, keep the petals loose on the last rows by not pressing the petals as tightly to the center.

shedding lace

TOYING WITH TEXTURE in sugar sculpture has always captivated me. In this cake, the smoothness of the fondant-covered tiers plays off the various layers of lace-imprinted fondant pieces.

A silicone mold was used to create the lace texture on this beauty's thin fondant layers, similar to the technique used to fabricate the brooches on the cake on page 232.

TO MAKE THE FONDANT PIECES, cut out medium to large circles from thinly rolled fondant then cut them in half with a knife to create semi-circles. Cover the semi-circles with a damp tea towel wrapped in plastic wrap (see page 134) to prevent them from drying out. Working with one at a time, press the fondant onto a lace mold dusted with cornstarch. Apply the pieces directly to the fondant-covered cake, using a mixture of corn syrup and water to secure them. Overlap the fondant pieces to achieve a layered, textured look.

For extra special occasions, before you add the textured lace decorations, mix edible gold dust with vodka to form a paintable liquid, then brush it directly onto the chilled iced or fondant-covered cake tiers with an oversized brush. Paint the top layers of the lace decoration with this gold mixture as well.

boho ruffles

STACKING CAKE TIERS OFF CENTER creates more room on the ledges to place decorations, or it can also produce an unexpected look if you leave the ledges bare. Here, the combination of the off-centered tiers and various ruffled textures produces a romantic, fresh sensation as your eyes move around the striking layers.

TO TIER AN OFF-CENTERED CAKE, follow the steps on pages 120 to 123, but instead of centering all the straws, insert them off-center, where the next cake will be placed. It's still helpful to use a cake board to trace the positioning of the straws, so that they will be even in diameter. Insert a center dowel through the entire cake, orienting it through the center of the bottom tier.

TO CREATE THE APPLIQUÉ ON THIS CAKE, which is inspired by the way birch bark dramatically curls and naturally strips off its trunk, cut various sized strips out of thinly rolled white sugar paste. With a utility knife, cut fringe on either side of the strips, then ruffle the edges using a small ball tool. Attach the pieces to the cake tiers, using a mixture of equal parts water and corn syrup as glue and applying the ruffles in different directions, layering some on top of one another for added depth and texture. To add more dimension to the ruffles, gently dry dust the edges using a soft paintbrush and a mixture of ivory and brown powder dyes.

Sculpting Feathers

When sculpting sugar feathers, let your creativity guide you. The more unique the shapes and sizes, the more realistic the feathers will appear. Instead of using feather cutters, I use a utility knife and cut feather shapes freehand. Here, the feathers are in neutral tones, but they can be made in vibrant colors as well.

TOOLS:

- cornstarch in a muslin bag for dusting
- silicone rolling pin
- neutral-toned Sugar Paste (page 59)
- damp tea towel wrapped in plastic wrap (see page 134)
- utility knife
- foam pad
- small-medium ball tool
- veining tool
- 20-gauge wire trimmed to 8-inch lengths
- 1:1 mixture of water and corn syrup
- fruit carton for drying
- paintbrush
- powder dyes

❶ On a cornstarch-dusted surface using the silicone rolling pin, roll out the sugar paste to a thickness of $1/16$ inch. Rotate the paste evenly as you roll out, as you would for a piecrust. If the sugar paste begins to stick, dust more cornstarch on the surface. Cover any sugar paste you are not using with the plastic-wrapped tea towel to prevent the sugar paste from drying out.

❷ Using the utility knife, cut out at least 10 different sized feather shapes from the sugar paste. Place them inside the tea towel to prevent the sugar paste from drying out.

❸ Working with one at a time, place a feather on a cornstarch-dusted foam pad and use the ball tool to thin and ruffle the edges.

❹ Still working on the foam pad, use the veining tool to lightly mark a line down the center of the feather, then make lines from the center angled diagonally upwards to create the feather's veins.

❺ Working on a nonstick surface, use the utility knife to cut the edges of the feather to create fringe.

6 Place the feather back on the foam pad, and using the ball tool, thin out the edges, rolling the edges in small back-and-forth motions to create rough, ruffled edges.

7 Dip the end of the wire into the water and corn syrup mixture to coat it with a modest amount.

8 Press the damp end of the wire in the center of the feather, extending from the bottom about one-quarter of the height of the feather.

9 Lightly pinch the underside of the feather onto the wire so that the wire does not show.

10 Set the feather on a fruit carton to dry, arranging it in an organic shape. Let the feathers dry for at least 48 hours before continuing. To finish, use the paintbrush and powder dyes to dry-dust each feather with darker and iridescent shades. For reddish-brown feathers, I like to use raspberry or beet powder.

mushroom forest

MAKING A SMALL TIERED CAKE can turn even an intimate gathering into a memorable event. For this one, a tree slab stand is a fun prop that adds to the rustic effect. Pair the Espresso Icing on page 68 with sugar paste mushrooms in warm tones to give the cake a natural quality. For a spackled-looking finish, crisscross the icing in an organic pattern with a mini spatula or a spoon.

THESE LIGHTHEARTED AND FANCIFUL MUSHROOMS can easily be geared towards kids or adults. You can sculpt them with sugar paste or marzipan in realistic earthy tones or bright colors. Here I've created an ombré effect with the color of the mushrooms descending from a pale yellow to a deep mustard. This adds a fun twist to an already whimsical idea, while keeping the overall design simple.

Sculpting Mushrooms

When sculpting mushrooms, I like to alternate the stems and caps with a variety of shapes and colors for a playful yet natural feel. For the mushrooms shown on this cake, mix five different yellow and neutral-toned shades of sugar paste. Individually wrap them in plastic wrap to prevent the sugar paste from drying out. I often use sandwich bags when sculpting with multiple colors for easy storage. When you're done, you can save them to reuse for your next project.

TOOLS:

- cornstarch in a muslin bag for dusting
- Sugar Paste (page 59) tinted to desired colors
- 20-gauge wire cut into 2-inch lengths
- Styrofoam cake dummy for drying the mushrooms
- ball tool
- veining tool
- parchment paper
- baking sheet
- 1:1 mixture of water and corn syrup
- paintbrush and powder dyes

❶ For each mushroom, start with a grape-size amount of sugar paste and sculpt it into a log that is slightly tapered at one end to create the mushroom stem—the log shapes can be fat and short or slender and tall. Make a mixture of both for a variety. Once you've sculpted a variety of stems, insert a wire down the center of each, trimming the wire to leave an extra ½ inch on one end. This will come in handy when drying the mushrooms and will keep them stable when arranging them on the cake. Set aside in the cake dummy to dry.

2 To sculpt the mushroom caps, start with an assortment of pea- to grape-size balls of sugar paste. Use your fingers and/or a ball tool to make a variety of shapes from roundead cones to shallow umbrella caps, hollowing out the underside in order to fit them over the stems.

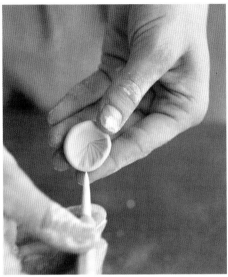

3 Using the veining tool, lightly mark gills on the undersides of the mushroom caps. Set the caps on a parchment-lined baking sheet, and let the mushroom stems and caps dry for 24 to 48 hours.

4 Dab a small amount of water–corn syrup mixture inside the caps.

5 Attach the caps to the stems, combining the different colors, shapes, and sizes for a fun mix. Place in the cake dummy to dry for at least 4 hours. To give the mushrooms depth, dry-dust them with neutral and yellow powder dyes. I also like to dust cocoa powder on the edges for a natural dirt look. When applying on a cake for decoration, place the mushroom stem onto the cake, securing it in place with the wire.

sugar fans

A DRAMATICALLY TALL CAKE TIER deserves an incredible, unique design. These fans were created from hand-cut forms of rolled sugar paste pressed into a silicone mold I made myself (although you can use any store-bought lace texture mold).

A few summers ago at the Brooklyn Flea, I bonded with a vendor over our love of antique fabric and walked out an hour later with a box of lace she passed on to me at an incredible bargain. At the time, I was experimenting with making silicone molds, and it only seemed fitting to make use of one of those beautiful lace pieces. To this day I find this lace pattern sneaking its way into many of my cake designs.

THESE FANS CAN BE CREATED WITH ANY TYPE of large lace mold: see page 332 for resources. By hand, cut teardrop shapes out of thinly rolled sugar paste in a variety of colors, and then press each one individually onto a mold to imprint it with a lace pattern. Let the pieces dry on a flat surface for 48 hours to 1 week before handling. Once dry, use a modest amount of royal icing on the underside to adhere various groupings in a fan shape, overlapping each piece.

To cover the unfinished bottom edges of the fans, make a few sugar paste buttons or brooches in similar colors (see page 234) and attach them in clusters using royal icing. Let the assembled fans dry overnight. Once the royal icing is dry, the fans and buttons can be dry-dusted using a paintbrush and iridescent powders to highlight the different textures.

iridescent black

MUCH OF WHAT I CREATE is derived from nature in one form or another. These velvety blooms were inspired by blue-black double hellebores, flowers that are rare to find growing in nature.

TO MAKE THE HELLEBORES, follow instructions for making petals on a wire on page 148, using small and large teardrop cutters to cut out smooth, round petals from dark purple sugar paste. Lightly transfer veins onto the petals using a silicone vein mold. Allow petals to dry in a fruit carton for at least 48 hours to 1 week. Once dry, use brown floral tape to arrange 10 to 12 small petals around a small bunch of black stamens, followed by 5 to 6 larger petals. Using a paintbrush and black and light purple powder dye, dry-dust the edges of the petals and over the veins to create highlights and shadows.

Covering cakes in fondant allows more flexibility in the coloring, so you can achieve dark, artificial colors. When I want to achieve a dark finishing color, I'll often use fondant over icing so there is only a very thin layer of the dark color with plain icing underneath. In this case, the bottom tier is a dark purple, black hue. The white tier on top is painted with edible silver dust that has been mixed with vodka; the bottom tier is lightly dusted with dry silver dust to accent the top tier. Placing such a drastically lighter, reflective color on top of the black tier accentuates the dark flowers.

wild artichoke

WHEN DECORATING A CAKE with a large focal point, such as this dramatic artichoke, keep the rest of the cake soft and simple so the sugar sculpture can shine on its own. To make the antique-looking ivory icing, add a few drops of dark espresso to the Madagascar Vanilla Bean Icing on page 66. I used a spoon to create a casual swirled texture.

WHEN SCULPTING LARGE FORMS, use an oversized Styrofoam ball attached with royal icing to a hooked wire as the base to reduce the weight of the final product. Begin by cutting out small, narrow purple sugar paste leaves and adhering them with a mixture of equal parts water and corn syrup to the Styrofoam ball. Continue to apply the leaves in layers, letting them dry overnight after every few layers. To resemble a realistic artichoke, make the sugar leaves toward the center a deep purple. Then, as you make your way towards the outer layers of the bulb, switch to a deep green sugar paste and continue layering, using a larger leaf cutter for the outer leaves. Because it is such a large sculpture, allow it to dry for 1 to 2 weeks. While the artichoke is drying, create deep green sugar paste leaves on wires following the instructions on page 152, and apply them to the bottom of the artichoke bulb with green floral tape for an incredibly realistic feel. Once the artichoke is done, dry-dust the leaves using a paintbrush and deep purple and green powder dyes, mixing the colors where the purple and green leaves meet to enhance the transition between colors.

brooch flowers

FOR A FUN AND EASY FINISH, alternate cake tiers with different icing textures and colors. Here, I combined a smooth white icing with a roughly striped peach hued one, using a mini spatula to create the stripes. Flower ornaments, made by pressing tinted sugar paste into silicone button or brooch molds (instructions follow), are enhanced with gray sugar paste leaves (see page 152) and silver sugar paste balls.

I like to use pomegranate powder, cherry powder, strawberry powder, and edible gold dust for dry-dusting and adding definition to details. For more gold highlights, mix gold dust with vodka until soupy and all the lumps have dissipated, then use a fine-tip brush to paint accents on the sugar brooches.

TO MAKE THE SILVER SUGAR PASTE BALLS, roll a pea-size amount of gray sugar paste in the palm of your hand. Let the ball dry overnight before dusting with edible silver dust.

Sculpting Brooches from Molds

This cake's sugar brooches, which resemble abstract flowers, were created using silicone molds, which are great for making detailed sugar objects in high volume in little time. I always use sugar paste, not fondant or marzipan, when using these types of molds so that the sculptures hold the shape and texture of the impression. The molds can be bought at various online cake decorating stores (see Resources, page 332). Although silicone molds are a bit of an investment, they will last for ages with proper care and will help add that unique value to your cake designs.

TOOLS:

- coral and peach-toned Sugar Paste (page 59)
- brooch or button silicone molds
- cornstarch in a muslin bag for dusting
- utility knife
- damp tea towel wrapped in plastic wrap (see page 134)
- small and large paintbrush
- variety of pink and coral powdered dyes
- FDA-certified gold dust
- vodka

❶ Knead various coral hues of sugar paste on a nonstick surface to bring to room temperature. Keep the pieces individually wrapped to prevent them from drying out. Lightly dust the silicone molds with cornstarch to prevent the sugar paste from sticking.

❷ Portion out the amount of sugar paste it takes to fill one mold at a time. The sugar paste should fill to a little less than the top of the mold. Once you've found the right amount to fill the mold, roll the sugar paste into a ball until there are no creases. Gently press the sugar paste evenly into the mold, keeping the edges within the mold. This will help the sugar paste pick up the minute details of the mold.

❸ Release the sugar paste from the mold, handling cautiously to avoid dulling any of the detail. Assuming the mold was dusted with cornstarch, the sugar paste should come out easily. If the shape isn't releasing, gently squeeze the flexible mold back and forth until the shape becomes loose enough to remove.

❹ Use the utility knife or your fingers to soften any rough edges.

❺ Use a variety of brooch molds, alternating colors to make multiple coral shades per mold. Allow the sugar pieces to dry for at least 48 hours before painting and handling. Dry-dust the brooches using a paintbrush and pink and coral powders. Use a small brush to finish off details with painted accents of gold dust mixed with vodka.

dripping pearls

WHEN DECORATING WITH OVERSIZED SUGAR FLOWERS, like this Bayahibe rose, little additional decoration is needed as you want to allow the blooms to naturally be center stage.

Ball sprinkles are a great way to add a little extra pop of design or color in an effortless way. Here they are positioned to resemble a dripping string of pearls. To make metallic hues, combine powder dye with a few drops of vodka in a bowl, add the sprinkles, and stir gently until the sprinkles are fully colored. Apply the sprinkles to a cake with tweezers for a deliberate design or simply toss them on for a more casual accent.

TO RE-CREATE THIS OVERSIZED BAYAHIBE ROSE, follow the instructions for making petals on wire on page 148, using light pink sugar paste. Here, I added extra petals to create a dramatically large rose.

~ ⑧ ~

modern

Departing from traditional styles opens
a window to endless creations.

When approaching modern cake design, you'll begin to notice the repetition of sharp edges, lines, and patterns, not only within the decorations on the cake but also in the physical shape of the cakes themselves. This aspect is what makes the act of creating modern cakes less romantic and more logical. Consistency is a must when crafting a repeating pattern. Making such analytical movements can seem laborious at first, but I always find it fascinating that when incorporating unconventional color schemes and shapes, the most controlled patterns can sometimes seem the most animated.

mosaic sea foam

THIS TILE-COVERED CREATION came from my passion for the sea: The green and blue water that swirls with white waves always amazes me. In this cake, the sea foam hues and sandcastle feel of the tiles and flags allude to a subtle ocean theme.

TO CREATE A MARBLED EFFECT IN FONDANT, twist together coils of fondant in multiple hues and white, then knead lightly. Roll out as usual. Marbled fondant (or sugar paste) can only be used once before losing its effect.

The sugar paste tiles are created using the same marbling technique as the fondant, in shades of light blue and green. Roll the sugar paste to a thickness of ⅛ inch and cut into small squares. Allow the squares to dry for at least 48 hours so they won't lose their shape when handled. Attach the squares to the cake using royal icing.

Sculpting Sugar Flags

Sugar flags are a simple way to top off any cake or dessert with something festive. They can also be made of paper if you're on the fly, but when they're made of sugar it adds an extra dreamy edible flair. They keep well when stored in an airtight container in a cool environment. I like to make extra to have on hand for a last minute cake or pie accent for an easy and impressive touch!

TOOLS:

- white Sugar Paste (page 59)
- cornstarch in a muslin bag for dusting
- silicone rolling pin
- damp tea towel wrapped in plastic wrap (see page 134)
- utility knife
- fine-tip paintbrush
- 1:1 mixture of water and corn syrup
- 18-gauge wire trimmed to 7-inch lengths
- fruit carton for drying
- vibrant or sparkle powder dye
- vodka

❶ Knead a plum-size amount of sugar paste on a nonstick surface to bring to room temperature. Dust your surface with cornstarch. Using the silicone rolling pin, roll out the sugar paste to a thickness of $1/16$ inch. Rotate the paste evenly as you roll out, as you would for a piecrust. If the sugar paste begins to stick, dust more cornstarch on the surface. Cover with the plastic-wrapped tea towel to prevent the sugar paste from drying out.

❷ Use the utility knife to cut out a variety of long triangular shapes. I like to cut these out by hand so each one is completely different.

❸ Place the triangles in the tea towel as you work to prevent the sugar paste from drying out.

❹ Use the fine-tip brush to apply the water–corn syrup mixture to the base of a triangle.

❺ Place a wire about ¹/₁₆ inch from the edge. Fold the edge over the wire and press gently.

❻ Set each flag on a fruit carton, letting waves form in the flags, and let dry for 48 hours.

❼ To finish, paint the wires with a vibrant color or metallic sparkle made by mixing powder dye with vodka.

❽ Insert the flags into the cake to the desired height.

❾ If needed, touch up the wires with the paint mixture.

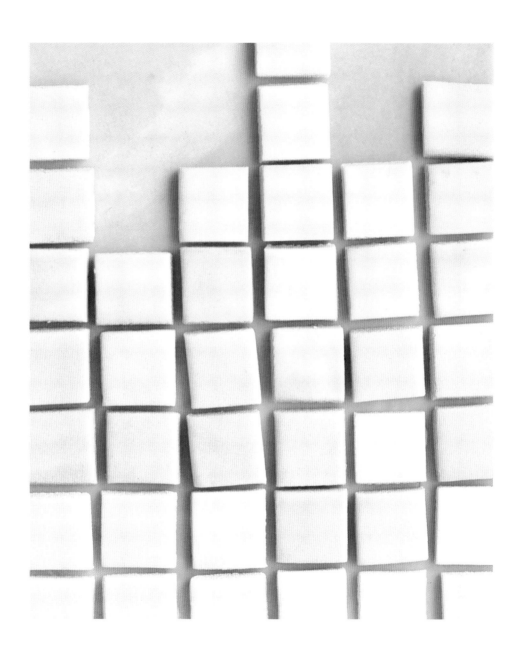

chevron motif

IN CURRENT CONTEMPORARY DESIGN, there's been a chevron craze. The familiar pattern is repeated time and again in various applications, especially in fashion and textiles. I for one am a huge fan. From one of its earliest sightings in ancient pottery to its more current use in military symbols, flags, and clothing—a chevron pattern is a powerful symbol that can be used in a variety of colors for a bold design. In this cake, I section the fondant chevron pattern in an uneven arrangement so that the yellow and white hues bounce off each other in a playful style. You could also space the stripes evenly and align them for a more traditional chevron pattern.

Creating and Applying a Chevron Pattern

This design can be made with a two-tone color combination as I did, or feel free to experiment with a few different colors for the chevron stripes and background. For multiple cake tiers, each tier can alternate with a different color pattern.

TOOLS:

- yellow and white Fondant (page 57)
- powdered sugar in a muslin bag for dusting
- silicone rolling pin
- 2 damp tea towels wrapped in plastic wrap (see page 134)
- pastry wheel or utility knife
- ruler
- 1:1 mixture of water and corn syrup
- paintbrush

❶ Knead the yellow fondant on a nonstick surface to bring to room temperature. Dust your surface with powdered sugar. Using the silicone rolling pin, roll out the fondant into a rectangular shape about ¹/₁₆ inch thick. Rotate the fondant evenly as you roll, as you would for a piecrust. If the fondant begins to stick, dust more powdered sugar on the surface. Cover with a plastic-wrapped tea towel to prevent the fondant from drying out.

❷ Use the pastry wheel or utility knife and the ruler to cut the fondant into a rectangle, so that the height is the same height as the cake tier you'll be applying the design to. For instance, this cake tier is 6 inches tall, so the height of the fondant rectangle is also 6 inches.

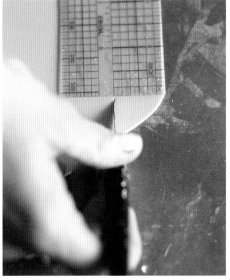

❸ Using the utility knife or pastry wheel and the ruler, trim the rectangle vertically into 1-inch strips. Cover the strips with the plastic-wrapped tea towel to prevent the fondant from drying out. Cut as many strips as you can get from the rolled out piece of fondant and set aside, covered. Depending on the circumference of the cake tier, you might have to roll out more, but work with what you have to get started. Because fondant dries out so quickly, I find it easier to work with small quantities at a time.

❹ Knead the white fondant on a nonstick surface to bring to room temperature. Dust your surface with powdered sugar. Using the silicone rolling pin, roll out the fondant into a rectangle about $1/16$ inch thick. Rotate the fondant evenly as you roll, as you would for a piecrust. If the fondant begins to stick, dust more powdered sugar on the surface. Cover with a plastic-wrapped tea towel to prevent from drying out.

❺ Using the pastry wheel or utility knife and the ruler, trim the fondant into 2-inch strips in varying widths, from $1/4$ inch to $3/4$ inch. Cover the strips with a plastic-wrapped tea towel as you work to prevent the fondant from drying out. Set aside.

6 Remove one of the 1-inch yellow strips from the tea towel and set it on your work surface. Lightly dot a white strip with the water–corn syrup mixture with the brush.

7 Apply the white strip, wet side down, diagonally across the yellow strip. Repeat with additional white strips, brushing them with the water–corn syrup mixture and spacing them randomly to create a sporadic pattern.

8 Use the pastry wheel or utility knife to trim the strips to create a flush edge on each side.

9 If applying to a fondant cake, dot the back of the fondant strip with the water–corn syrup mixture to adhere it to the side of the cake tier. If applying to an iced cake, place directly on the chilled icing.

10 Apply the strip to the cake vertically. Repeat, placing each 1-inch strip flush with the previous one and alternating the angle of the stripes each time to create a chevron pattern.

neoclassical

THIS PATTERN WAS INSPIRED by 18th-century baroque and rococo patterns as well as my husband Scott's artwork, which features immaculate and detailed patterns and repetition. I don't have quite as much patience as he holds in a paintbrush, but I am moved by the concept of fabricating an ornate design freehand. Here, rather than painting a pattern on a canvas, I crafted my design out of fondant, carefully applying pieces to a fondant-covered cake.

After deciding on a design, make a pattern on a piece of graph paper at full scale. Cut out the pattern and use the pieces as a stencil to cut out thinly rolled fondant. For designs that need a certain amount of precision, I find it is also helpful to create a full-scale sketch of the entire design on graph paper to act as a reference for placing the pieces. You'll have more control over the placement of the design on a fondant-covered cake. To attach the fondant design, dab a small amount of a mixture of equal parts water and corn syrup to the backside of the pieces.

beyond polka dots

WHEN AN EDITOR from a wedding magazine whom I work with closely asked me to design a cake involving polka dots, I couldn't think of a better way to introduce a fresh interpretation of the commonly expected polka dot motif. This cake would also be a great alternative to the typical baby shower cake that has cut-out pink or blue fondant circles pasted all over it. These 3-D sugar paste circles are simple to create and bring a lively movement to a cake's design.

This design could be created on a round cake, but the hexagon shape of the tiers shown here produces interesting shapes and shadows with the circles. Continuing the pattern upwards in the toppers creates the illusion that the circles are floating.

Sculpting 3-D Circles

By molding the edges of what was an ordinary sugar paste circle into a cup shape, you can add a 3-D quality for added volume. Arrange them in a uniform fashion as I did on this cake, or place them on the cake more randomly for an organic feel.

TOOLS:

- light green Sugar Paste (page 59)
- cornstarch in a muslin bag for dusting
- silicone rolling pin
- damp tea towel wrapped in plastic wrap (see page 134)
- small circle cutters or large pastry tips
- foam board
- small-medium ball tool
- baking sheet
- parchment paper
- paintbrush
- powder dye
- Royal Icing (page 64)

❶ Knead a plum-size amount of sugar paste on a nonstick surface to bring to room temperature. Dust your surface with cornstarch. Using the silicone rolling pin, roll out the sugar paste to a thickness of ¹/₁₆ inch. Rotate the paste evenly as you roll, as you would for a piecrust. If the sugar paste begins to stick, dust more cornstarch on the surface. Cover with the plastic-wrapped tea towel to prevent the sugar paste from drying out.

❷ Cut out circles using a variety of small to medium cutters. You can also use a large round pastry tip. Place each one in the plastic-wrapped tea towel as you work.

❸ Working with one at a time, place a circle on a cornstarch-dusted foam board. Use the small ball tool to make gentle circular motions to thin out the circle while creating a cup shape. I encourage working these circles as thin as you can—the more translucent the circles, the more luminous the overall cake will appear. Place the shaped circles on a baking sheet lined with parchment paper and let dry for at least 48 hours.

❹ Dust the edges of the circles with turmeric (or any desired powder dye) for a contemporary look. To apply to a fondant cake, dab the circles with a small dot of royal icing. If applying to an iced cake, use a small amount of the same icing as the cake.

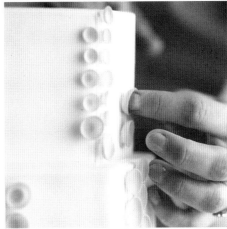

❺ Gently press the circles onto the cake. With such a small amount of icing, they should set very quickly.

Sculpting 3-D Circle Toppers

The 3-D circle decorations can be a fun detail on their own, but the topper adds an extra dimension to this cake. To create this seamless looking topper, work with the same sugar paste hue that is used to create the 3-D circles.

TOOLS:

- silicone rolling pin
- light green Sugar Paste (page 59)
- small round pastry tip (#01)
- damp tea towel wrapped in plastic wrap (see page 134)
- small paintbrush
- 1:1 mixture of water and corn syrup
- 24-gauge wire
- Royal Icing (page 64)

❶ Knead and roll out a small handful of sugar paste as you did to make the circles, then use the small pastry tip to cut out circles, placing each one in the tea towel as you work.

❷ Working with two circles at a time, dot each one with the water–corn syrup mixture.

❸ Sandwich the two circles on a wire with the wet sides facing each other. Press lightly and lay on a flat surface. Repeat this step a few times on each wire, making sure to cover the top of each wire with dots so the end doesn't show. Vary the number of dots on each wire in a random pattern. Let dry for 24 hours.

❹ Apply a small amount of royal icing to each dot; attach a 3-D circle (page 258) to each dot. Place the larger circles near the bottom of the wire, getting smaller towards the top. Let dry for 24 hours before using.

pleated angles

WHEN I WORK WITH A BRIDE to create a custom wedding cake, I often pull inspiration from her dress. It's important to me to incorporate something personal in each cake that I create, even if it's a minute detail. These details are what make someone's experience with a cake something extraordinary. This pattern originated from one client's wedding dress and has since transformed through many different cakes.

TO CREATE THIS EFFECT, layer long strips of thinly rolled fondant on a fondant-covered cake: Place the first strip around the base of a tier and attach it with a mixture of equal parts water and corn syrup. Add each next strip above the one below it, overlapping slightly. After layering strips about three-quarters of the way up the cake, apply stacks of several layered fondant triangles. Then continue adding horizontal strips until you reach the top. Play around with different color schemes depending on the occasion!

art deco emblems

AS A DETAIL-ORIENTED PASTRY CHEF, I absolutely love making art deco patterns on cakes! It seriously makes me the happiest to sit for hours making tiny decorations and applying them carefully until each one is in its place. These sugar paste fans, which are hand cut and shaped, can be applied while they're wet or dry. I waited for them to dry, so I could paint the bottoms gold and dust the edges with a bright purple powder dye to highlight the ridges (created with a veining tool) before applying them to the cake with royal icing.

bubblegum pop

THIS DESIGN CAN BE RE-CREATED in any color or size, using a variety of circle cutters to make a collage pattern. This cake was made with oval cake pans as a simple alternative to the traditional round cake (see Resources, page 333, for info on where to find unusually shaped cake pans). The bright magenta icing is Rose Water–Raspberry Icing (page 67) with some dried raspberry powder added to enhance the color. For this cake, I strained the raspberry puree so the icing would appear smooth without the seeds and pulp.

TO MAKE THE CIRCLES, cut out a variety of colored circles from rolled-out sugar paste, placing them in a damp tea towel wrapped in plastic wrap (see page 134) to keep them from drying out as you work. Cut out smaller circles from the centers of the larger circles and save the cut-out circles for accent dots. In some of the circles, simply make an imprint with the cutters. Paint or dust the sugar paste shapes before attaching them to the cake. Overlay all of the sizes and colors to make a fun collage of circles; attach them while they are still wet so that they will lay flush with the curves of the cake. If making this design on an iced cake, make sure to keep the cake chilled while working with it. The circles will adhere to the moisture of the icing. If you are attaching them to a fondant-covered cake, use royal icing or a mixture of equal parts water and corn syrup as glue.

triangle on triangle

PLAY ON SHAPES FOR A MOD LOOK: In this case, a 3-D triangular cake is adorned with a 2-D triangle banner motif. Cake pans are made in just about every shape and size, or, to create unusual cake shapes at home without special pans, trace the shape desired on parchment paper, place the parchment on top of the baked cakes, and trim carefully. If you're making a shape with straight edges, like these triangles, it is better to start with a square cake.

This cake is covered in white fondant so the edges appear extra crisp, allowing the even edges of the pattern to really pop. The pattern is made by cutting out pieces of fondant using a triangle cutter. You can apply them wet or dry. I applied them dry using royal icing as glue; if applying them while wet, use a mixture of equal parts water and corn syrup to adhere. Apply the triangles in straight rows around the cake, skipping one at random and two underneath it to create a larger triangle outline in the fondant. While the color scheme is mostly pale pinks with hints of mustard yellow and orange, for an unexpected twist, on one side the brighter orange triangles are the dominant color.

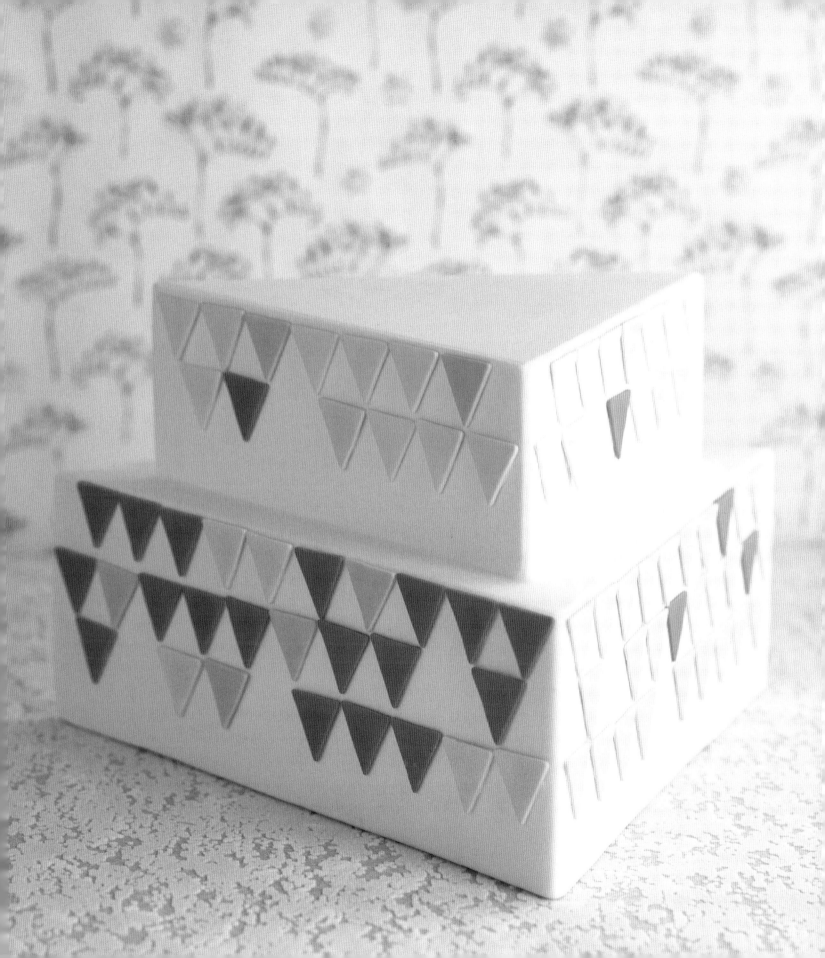

edible pop

SIMPLE TOOLS I have around the kitchen inspire many of the designs I create. Instead of going out and buying new gadgets, look around and try making a pattern or design from things you have at hand. For example, after stacking tiered cakes, I end up with a slew of dowel rod scraps I never know what to do with. When I wanted to achieve a stamped circle pattern, voilà! The end of a scrap dowel, used like a stamp, was the answer. Never feel like you have to own all the fancy tools to create something beautiful.

The design on this cake is drawn from styles used in the pop art movement of the 1960s, which featured flat, layered imagery and simple color schemes. I pasted bright fondant blossom and leaf cutouts on top of the stamped dots to add dimension but still keep the effect of a flat canvas. The graphic black stripes on the bottom tier, which balance the busyness of the top two tiers, are cut from thinly rolled pieces of fondant and then carefully applied with a mixture of equal parts water and corn syrup.

Painting Dots

This technique can be used to paint circles in a variety of sizes, colors, and patterns depending on the size of the dowel and the color of the dye. Here, I used Chefmaster's black natural food coloring. This technique works best on a fondant cake. To apply dots as shown on the pop art cake, paint the dots in vertical rows, staggering the dots with each row. I eyeball the placement, so the finished look is graphic and imperfect.

TOOLS:

- small dowel
- black or dark colored liquid dye
- paper towels

❶ Dip the end of the dowel into the dye. Dab off any excess dye on the edge of the bowl or a paper towel.

❷ Lightly press the end of the dowel onto a fondant-covered cake to create a dot. While applying the dots, hold a piece of parchment paper or a paper towel over the cake to avoid dripping on it.

❸ Repeat to make your desired pattern. Refresh the dowel with new dye each time to make a clean dot.

shooting stars

I'M A HUGE COLLECTOR of all things little. I'm running out of surfaces to fill! I'd like to thank (or blame) my dad for this. California raisin figurines, fruit- and vegetable-head salt and pepper shakers, antique bird wind-up toys—his collections are endless and fill his cabinets with unusual and inspiring imagery. I love the idea of collecting little things from your travels to keep with you as a continual reminder of those experiences. I discovered these gold paper decals in an antique store in Maine where there were treasures stacked floor to ceiling. I kept them stored in a small box in a drawer for years, not knowing that they would eventually become part of a cake. When decorating with special items that you wish to keep or reuse, use them only on a fondant-covered cake, not an iced cake, which would be too messy. Use royal icing to affix the paper decorations (or tchotchkes) to the cake, and gently remove them before serving.

9

modern
whimsy

Some of my favorite designs
are playful and a little relaxed.

*D*epending on the occasion, it can be nice to take some of the "preciousness" out of traditional cake decorating, move beyond your comfort zone, and let your designs evolve into something more transformative. This is one of my favorite aspects of making cakes!

Without getting too sentimental, I have to say: Cakes have a short moment of existence and then they're gone. Creatively, this allows you to move on, develop your ideas further, and create something new each time. I don't precisely reproduce any of my designs, so no one cake is the same as another. But they do tend to influence one another. The following cakes represent a state of playful maturity, as they were inspired by the designs and skill sets demonstrated in the previous chapters, yet they have distinctive styles of their own.

papier de fleur

PAPER FLOWERS that I make from dyed coffee filters accent this cake for an unusual texture. Paper flowers are a great alternative to sugar flowers, as they are more durable in warm weather and are easy to reuse if decorating a fondant cake.

Alternating different styles of cake tiers makes a modern design feel more fanciful. Here I've alternated fondant-covered hexagon tiers with round ones. For an even dreamier feel, paint on a cross-hatch pattern using a fine-tip paintbrush and yellow powder dye mixed with vodka. To play up the whimsical quality, I painted the pattern by hand for an imperfect look. This pattern can be painted on a chilled iced cake, but I prefer to apply it to a fondant-covered cake for a cleaner application.

TO MAKE PAPER FLOWERS, start with a handful of dry unbleached coffee filters. Mix a few drops of all-natural dye into a large bowl filled halfway with water. Drop a handful of filters into the water and let sit for about 1 minute, then wring out and set aside to dry overnight. Once dry, use a utility knife to cut petals in various sizes and shapes from the colored paper. Carefully layer the petal pieces around a wire, securing them with floral tape. To create a flower center, secure yellow stamens around a piece of wire with floral tape and then continue to layer the petals around the flower center. To create small flowers such as the yellow blossoms on the cake, simply wrap the petals around the wire without a center. Cut out leaves various sizes as well. Once you've created enough flowers and leaves, arrange them together in bunches and secure with floral tape.

candied gem

I'D LIKE TO THINK OF THIS CAKE as an edible geode rock, with light reflecting through the cavities of sparkling rock candy in two translucent colors, attached to a vivid purple fondant-covered cake. Making rock candy by hand is not only a fun science experiment, but also lets you control the size and color of the crystals; you could also use store-bought rock candy if you don't have the time or the desire to make your own. Cut the sugar crystals from the twine and crush them into the desired size pieces before applying the candy with royal icing to the surface of the cake. (If you are applying a lot of rock candy, as on this cake, allow the first layer of rock candy and royal icing to dry before layering on more, so that the candy won't fall off.) Accent the edges by painting them with edible gold dust mixed with vodka to give the candy the glistening appearance that geodes often have.

Crystals suitable to eat will form in about an hour and continue to grow for several days or even several weeks. If you do not see any crystals form during the first hour, something is wrong and you'll have to start over. Although you may see quick results in small measure, the larger rock candy crystals you're accustomed to seeing in the candy store will take at least 2 or 3 weeks to form.

Rock Candy

MAKES ABOUT 6 TO 8 ROCK CANDY STRINGS

4 cups evaporated cane juice

1 cup water

Natural liquid food coloring of choice

① In a medium saucepan, heat 2 cups of the evaporated cane juice and the water over medium heat, but do not boil. Stir until the evaporated cane juice is completely dissolved.

② Gradually add a few drops of the food coloring and the additional 2 cups evaporated cane juice, stirring continuously until all the evaporated cane juice is dissolved. Pour the solution into 6 to 8 clean, medium-size jars to fill three-quarters of the way full.

③ Cut baker's twine into 6-inch lengths, one for each jar. Tie each piece of twine to a pencil and suspend them across the mouth of the jars so that the ends hang into the syrup. Do not allow the twine to touch to bottom or edge of the jar.

④ Once crystals form to the size of your liking (anywhere from days to weeks), gently remove the pencil and string from the jar and lay the rock candy on paper towels to soak up the extra moisture. Once dry, cut the crystals off the twine. Store the rock candy in an airtight container in a dry environment for up to 6 months.

piñata

PIÑATAS HAVE MATURED QUITE A BIT since I was a kid. You can now find many piñata shapes beyond the traditional donkey, often in hip colors and metallic finishes. So, why not a completely edible piñata? This piñata cake is covered head to toe with fringed strips of fondant in muted green, dark teal, gray, and light blue. The tall-stacked cake tiers in different shapes and sizes create a multitude of spaces, curves, and edges to accent the fringe's versatile movement. You can re-create this piñata texture in any shape, color, or size. I would recommend using caution if smashing.

Creating and Applying Piñata Texture

TOOLS:

- powdered sugar in a muslin bag for dusting
- silicone rolling pin
- different colors Fondant (page 57)
- pastry wheel
- ruler
- damp tea towel wrapped in plastic wrap (see page 134)
- utility knife
- fine-tip paintbrush
- 1:1 mixture of water and corn syrup

❶ Dust your surface with powdered sugar. Using the silicone rolling pin, roll out the fondant into a rectangle $1/8$ inch to $1/16$ inch thick. Rotate the fondant evenly as you roll, as you would for a piecrust. If the fondant begins to stick, dust more powdered sugar on the surface.

❷ Use the pastry wheel and ruler to trim a 12-by-6-inch rectangle from the fondant.

❸ Use the pastry wheel and ruler to trim the rectangle into three 12-by-2-inch strips. Cover with the plastic-wrapped tea towel to prevent the fondant from drying out.

❹ Trim each strip into four 3-by-2-inch pieces, covering the pieces with the tea towel as you work.

❺ Work with one rectangle at a time. Use the utility knife to cut fringe on one long edge, leaving a ½-inch-wide section un-fringed on the top of the rectangle.

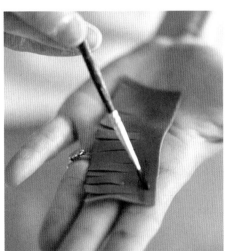

❻ To attach the pieces to a fondant-covered cake, use a fine-tip paintbrush to dot the back of the un-fringed edge with the water–corn syrup mixture. (Work with one strip at a time.) If applying to an iced cake, apply directly on the chilled icing without the water mixture.

❼ Apply to the cake one strip at a time, creating a complete row around the cake tier. Start from the bottom of the cake tier, and then add each row on top of another so that the fringe covers the un-fringed section of the piece underneath. Every now and then, alternate the colors of the rows to create a festive stripe pattern. To finish the top of the cake, continue layering the fringe in a circular pattern until it's completely covered.

gold in chaos

THIS DESIGN TESTS GRAVITY in such a way that you might forget that you're looking at a cake! The shape, inspired by a gold lamp, was a little too pristine on its own, so I accented it with sugar thistles.

TO MAKE AN UPSIDE-DOWN TIERED CAKE, insert straws into each tier following the instructions on page 120, with each tier on a cake board for stability. Stack the tiers from smallest to largest, then insert a wooden dowel as described on page 122. Since vegan, gluten-free cakes are more fragile than other cakes, I recommend stacking no more than three cakes, and keep them on the smaller size, with the top tier no larger than 8 inches in diameter. Fondant-covered cakes are great for a design such as this since the fondant acts as an outer shell to protect the tiers.

Here, I brushed the cake and boards lightly with a gold wash using a large paintbrush and gold dust mixed with vodka. For a more transparent metallic finish, add extra vodka to the gold wash.

TO MAKE THE THISTLES, follow the instructions for sculpting blossoms on a wire on page 142, using a daisy cutter and dark purple sugar paste and layering 10 to 15 rows of petals to create a rounded thistle shape. Follow the technique on page 152 to make the leaves, using a dark green sugar paste. I dry-dusted both the thistles and leaves with darker powder dyes to create shadows that contrast the gold tiers.

mod earth

A SWATCH OF 1960s-STYLE wallpaper inspired this cake. Like the original source, it uses basic shapes to create nature-themed imagery; translating part of the pattern into abstract 3-D plants further enlivens the design.

SUGAR PASTE SCULPTURE CAN BE MOLDED in a multitude of ways. To create these mod-looking flowers, start by simply shaping a brown sugar paste ball on a hooked wire, then attach cupped circles around the base. To make the sugar paste leaves, follow the instructions on page 152, using a narrow leaf cutter. The flat motif on the bottom tier is fondant cut out in dots, lines, and leaves and arranged to look like a flower.

Not only can you be creative with sugar paste shapes to produce unusual designs, but you can also utilize different color schemes. Picking three unique, muted colors for this design allowed the shapes to become the focal point.

magical grubs

WHEN SCULPTING IN SUGAR, the biggest challenge is to portray something that isn't meant to be still and create a sense of movement. I've found that movement is not only captured within each decoration itself but also in the arrangement of the cake design. These insects are layered around one another, with the wings overlapping the bodies, to create a natural flow. Placed on the sides of the tiers facing upward, they camouflage the edges of the tiers and appear to be moving purposefully. The insects' bodies are informed by my contemplation of bugs in nature, while the sparkling wings and unusual colors add a fanciful twist.

TO CREATE THE SOFTLY MUTED STRIPES AND DOTS on the fondant, make a very watered-down liquid by mixing a soft ivory powder dye with vodka. Paint on the fondant with a medium brush, using the edge of a piece of parchment paper and a circle cutter as a loose guide, although the edges of the lines and dots are meant to look faded and not precise. Let dry for a few minutes and then gently rub the edges with a cotton ball or paper towel for a very faded look.

Sculpting Insects

These insects are made of sugar paste with edible rice-paper wings. The translucent wings are painted with silver dust and attached to the bodies with royal icing.

TOOLS:

- different colors Sugar Paste (page 59)
- cornstarch in a muslin bag for dusting
- plastic wrap
- veining tool
- parchment paper
- baking sheet
- edible rice paper
- utility knife
- Royal Icing (page 64)
- fine-tip paintbrush
- FDA-certified edible silver dust
- vodka

❶ Knead a few different colorful hues of sugar paste on a cornstarch-dusted nonstick surface to bring to room temperature. Keep each piece wrapped in plastic wrap while working to prevent the sugar paste from drying out. Dust your hands lightly with cornstarch if the sugar paste feels sticky. Start with a grape-size amount of sugar paste, and sculpt it into a rounded cone shape to make the insect's body. Make different shapes and sizes for a variety of insects.

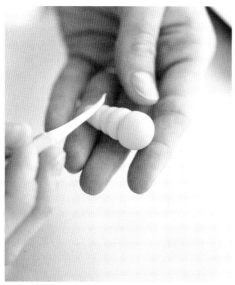

❷ Use a veining tool to create horizontal lines for the segments on the insect's body. Curve the tail and body in a subtle fashion. Place on a parchment-lined baking sheet to dry for 48 hours before applying the wings.

❸ To create the wings, trace or draw a different shaped set of mirrored wings per insect body onto edible rice paper. Handle with care—rice paper can be very brittle! Use a utility knife to cut out the traced wings. Use the first sets of wings as templates and cut out as many wings needed. Once the bug body has dried for at least 48 hours, dab a small amount of royal icing onto the center of the wings.

❹ Adhere the wings to the underside of the body. Press the wings gently up. Allow to dry for 24 hours against the inside edge of a sheet pan. To create veins on the wings, paint delicate lines with a fine-tip paintbrush and silver dust mixed with vodka. Use a small amount of royal icing to apply the bugs to a fondant-covered cake. If decorating an iced cake, use small dots of the same icing to keep the bugs in place.

a white cake

ORCHIDS HAVE ALWAYS BEEN a favorite flower to reproduce in sugar. I'm in love with not only their unique textures but also the intricacy of the details in the shapes they create. This cake is something extra dreamy: Using a combination of different sugar orchid species in a monotone color and layering them on top of each other allows the individual flowers to become an entirely different texture and shape as a whole.

Various orchid cultivars can be re-created in sugar paste using specialty orchid cutters, which you can find at cake decorating stores (or see page 332 for online resources). This is one instance where it's helpful to use specific cutters because the parts of an orchid are so intricate and unique. It's also a good idea to familiarize yourself with working with sugar paste by making simpler flowers on wires before attempting orchids.

TO CREATE A SUGAR PASTE ORCHID, you will need to make seven main parts: a center column, a main lip petal, and then two petals and three sepals to surround the lip. In addition, for this cake, you'll need a few pointed leaves to place around the orchids.

Make the center column first by sculpting a small, oblong shape on the end of a hooked wire. Allow this piece to dry for 48 hours to 1 week before using. Once it's dry, wrap the lip petal around the column, adhering it with a mixture of equal parts water and corn syrup. Let dry in a fruit carton for support and to keep the lip petal open. Make the 5 additional petals and sepals on wires, following the instructions on page 148 and using orchid cutters. Create varying sized leaves using the leaf technique on page 152, using orchid leaf cutters or cutting out the shapes by hand. Allow the lip petal, petals, sepals, and leaves to dry in fruit cartons for 48 hours to 1 week before assembling the orchids.

To assemble, place the petals and sepals around the lip petal and wrap the wires with floral tape. After arranging the orchids on the cake, place the leaves around the flowers as an accent.

flying pinwheels

TWO SQUARE CAKE TIERS sandwiching one tall round tier creates a windmill-like tower. The top tiers are covered in blue-green fondant for a matte look, and the white fondant base is decorated with pink fondant strips. Carefully apply the strips one at a time, affixing them to the cake with a mixture of equal parts water and corn syrup. Paper pinwheels finish the windmill effect. Glue them to straws or skewers. They make a simple decoration on a cake such as this, or they can also be used to decorate petite desserts such as cupcakes or even a pie! I doubled up two different sizes, gluing them together, to create more of a flower look.

TO MAKE THE PINWHEELS: Start with a paper square in any textile or pattern. If the pattern is only on one side, it will only show on part of the pinwheel. So before cutting and gluing the paper, make sure the side you want to show predominantly is facedown. Cut inward from each corner (on the diagonal), making sure to not cut all the way to the center. Bend one side of each corner toward the center to create a windmill shape and use a hot glue gun to secure the tips tightly at the center.

day of the dead

THIS FESTIVE CAKE was inspired by the Day of the Dead, the Mexican holiday celebrated in remembrance of passed loved ones. To honor them, people leave offerings such as sugar skulls or flowers at altars decorated with festive paper garlands made of *papel picado*. A traditional Mexican folk art commonly incorporated into religious and secular holiday decorations, *papel picado* ("perforated paper") features patterns hand-cut from paper by local artisans. I re-created similar garlands in sugar. The little skull figures on the cake would typically resemble and honor the deceased.

Making Sugar Garlands

Different colors symbolize specific holidays. The bright hues of these sugar paste garlands are in spirit of the Day of the Dead, but the flags of the garlands can be made in any desired color, shape, or pattern. I find it easier to create smaller garlands on short pieces of twine, rather than one long one, and attach the garland to the cake in multiple places with small pins.

TOOLS:

- different colors Sugar Paste (page 59)
- cornstarch in a cotton muslin bag for dusting
- silicone rolling pin
- damp tea towel wrapped in plastic wrap (see page 134)
- medium scalloped circle cutter
- pastry wheel
- mini petal cutters or a # 01 piping tip
- fine-tip paintbrush
- 1:1 mixture of water and corn syrup
- baker's twine
- soft modeling tool
- parchment paper
- baking sheet

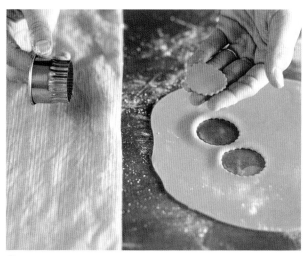

❶ Knead a small handful of sugar paste on a nonstick surface to bring to room temperature. Dust your surface with cornstarch. Using a silicone rolling pin, roll out the sugar paste to a thickness of ¹/₁₆ inch. Rotate the paste evenly as you roll, as you would for a piecrust. If the sugar paste begins to stick, dust more cornstarch on the surface. Cover with the plastic-wrapped tea towel to prevent the sugar paste from drying out. Use the medium circle cutter to cut circles from the sugar paste. Place each circle in the tea towel as you work to prevent the sugar paste from drying out.

❷ Working with one circle at a time, use the pastry wheel to trim ¼ inch off the circle to create a flag with a flat top. Trim a little, about ⅛ inch, off the sides so that only the bottom edge is rounded.

❸ Working swiftly and carefully, use the mini petal cutter or pastry tip to cut a pattern in the flag.

❹ Use the fine-tip paintbrush to dot the back top of the flag with the water–corn syrup mixture.

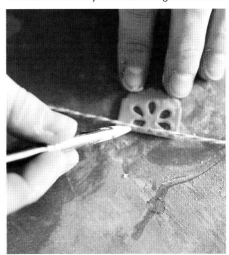

❺ Lay the baker's twine across the wet edge of the flag, with the flag in the center of the twine. Fold the top edge of the flag over the twine, pressing gently with a soft tool to close the seam.

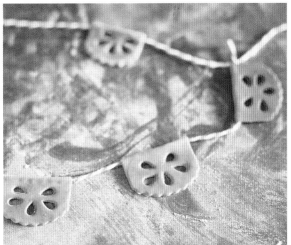

❻ Repeat this process, leaving about an inch between each flag, making sure the flags are all facing the same way. Alternate colors randomly for a playful pattern. Once you've attached the desired number of flags to the twine, place the garland on a parchment-lined baking sheet and let dry for 48 hours.

vintage tin

I ADORE keeping flowers around my apartment. The fresh smelling blooms and extra pops of color really make my day. It's the simple things, right? I'll often arrange them in containers such as vintage jars and tins, which is what inspired me to create this cake.

The cake is topped with a lush bouquet of sugar flowers and leaves, including double tulips, peonies, daisies, and miniature poppies. Follow the instructions on pages 138 to 155 to create different flowers on wires, blossoms, and leaves. When arranging large bouquets such as this, begin by carefully inserting the larger blooms first, then filling in with medium to smaller blossoms, and then finishing by filling in any empty spaces with leaves. Because the sugar flowers are on wires, you can carefully move them around to make small adjustments.

TO MAKE THE "TIN": Cover a round cake with orange fondant, then apply two gray strips of fondant around the top and one around the bottom to create the look of an antique tin. With a fine-tip paintbrush and edible silver dust mixed with vodka, paint the gray lines silver. Paint the detail of your choice on a rolled-out piece of ivory fondant (I painted the horse freehand, but you could also use a stencil as a guide), cut it out using an oval cutter, and apply it to the cake with a mixture of equal parts water and corn syrup. Apply a thin gray fondant strip around the edge of the oval and paint it silver as you did the other strips around the tin. To give the tin an all-over antique look, dry-dust the cake using a large soft paintbrush with silver dust and a mix of cocoa powder and cornstarch for a light ivory hue.

10

dessert
tables

Have fun with the way you display
your cakes and desserts.

reating a dessert table with different layers and multiple cakes and desserts produces an eclectic style and flavor palate that isn't possible with just one cake or dessert. A dessert table is an automatic showstopper at a party and allows for the guests to have an interactive play with the desserts.

On the following pages, you'll see the different characteristics a dessert table can exhibit, depending on the style of the cakes, the selection of other petite desserts, and the décor. My go-to desserts are mini tarts, coconut macaroons or chocolate truffles, cupcakes, and mini cakes. Depending on the season, you can accent the table with caramel-covered apples or even cookies.

Some of the visual elements that enhance a dessert table are linens, cake stands, plates, trays, serving utensils, and flowers. Vary the heights of the cakes and desserts by stacking cake stands on crates, boxes—even books. I especially enjoy adding flea market finds to the mix to create a beautiful, eclectic spread. I'll often arrange the props and cakes on the table first, and then place the desserts among the various elements.

Flowers can be displayed in various ways, such as a bouquet in a vase, as individual blooms loosely placed around the table, or even as a backdrop. For the following dessert tables, my dear friend Liza Lubell, who is the owner of Peartree Flowers in Brooklyn, created all of the floral elements.

blooming tangerines

ONE OF MY FAVORITE APPROACHES to designing a dessert table is blending cake designs as well as desserts together that don't necessarily share the same style or decorating techniques but have similar inventiveness and color hues: in this case, a mixture of contemporary patterns, rustic cakes, and mini tarts with fresh fruit. A wooden crate and cake stands are used to create platforms of varying heights for the desserts. I found this specific soda crate with my gram, Shirley, at an Amish market in rural Pennsylvania.

- **PAPIER DE FLEUR CAKE**
  (page 280)

- **CHEVRON MOTIF CAKE**
  (page 249)

- **TRIANGLE ON TRIANGLE CAKE**
  (page 268)

  >>>

- **SUGAR TARTS WITH LEMON CURD AND FRESH RASPBERRIES:** Bake the Sugar Tart Dough (page 328) in mini tartlet pans or mini cupcake tins. Fill the cooled tartlet shells with Lemon Curd (page 327) and top each one with a fresh raspberry.

- **SUGAR TARTS WITH STRAWBERRY-BASIL ICING AND CANDIED KUMQUATS:** Fill cooled tartlet shells with Strawberry-Basil Icing (page 67) and garnish each one with a candied kumquat (see Candied Citrus, page 329).

- **ORANGE-CARROT MINI CAKES:** Use a round cookie cutter to cut out circles of Orange-Carrot Cake (page 81). Layer the cake circles with apricot jam and Madagascar Vanilla Bean Icing (page 66), and garnish with candied kumquats or fresh raspberries. You can't go wrong with layering any flavor of cake with fresh jam and vanilla bean icing!

stormy
lavender

MOODY AND ROMANTIC stand three of my personal favorite cakes, which defy balance in more than one sense, and as a grouping create multifarious layers. The diverse cakes are carefully placed in such a way that no one takes center stage over another. Amid this trio, a variety of complementing petite desserts are scattered around the composition, creating a beautiful rhythm among the tablescape.

- GOLD IN CHAOS CAKE
  (page 290)

- SHEDDING LACE CAKE
  (page 215)

- CANDIED GEM CAKE
  (page 283)

  >>>

- **SUGAR TARTS WITH LAVENDER GANACHE:** Bake the Sugar Tart Dough (page 328) in small tartlet pans. Fill the cooled tartlet shells with Ganache (page 69) and then top each one with candied lavender (use lavender buds, and follow the instructions for Candied Citrus on page 329). The Caramel Sauce on page 331 also makes a wonderful filling for the sugar tarts.

- **TRUFFLES WITH CANDIED LAVENDER:** Follow the how-to on page 188 to make truffles. Use a small dot of ganache to attach a piece of candied lavender on top of each truffle.

- **MEXICAN CHOCOLATE CUPCAKES** (page 73) with Ginger Icing (page 68)

- **MEXICAN CHOCOLATE CUPCAKES** (page 73) with Espresso Icing (page 68)

rustic and refined

LIMITING THE AMOUNT OF COLOR in a design brings the focus more towards the form rather than the color. When I was in school in Vermont, I witnessed many vivid falls and winters. I was constantly blown away by how lively the landscape appeared during seasons of nearly dead foliage and a blanketed white environment. Simplicity can be undervalued, especially in cake design. In this tablescape, the natural tones and romantic lines create a warm movement that excites the eye. The subtle colors of the surrounding props and flowers continue the theme. The cakes and other desserts are set on muted pewter stands or stacked on top of tree stumps and other rustic platters. White and rusty orange flowers complement the warm colors of the sugar feathers on the Boho Ruffles cake (right), while the muted green leaves and budding branches soften the warm colors with their cool tones.

- A WHITE CAKE

  (page 299)

- BOHO RUFFLES CAKE

  (page 216)

- COCONUT MACAROONS

  (page 330)

- MINI ROUGH-ICED CAKES: Use round cookie cutters in a variety of sizes to cut out circles of Coconut Cake (page 85). Layer the cake pieces with Lemon Curd (page 327) and Ginger Icing (page 68). Crumb-coat the cakes with ginger icing following the instructions on page 112, then stack them into tiers (with such small cakes, there is no need for straws or dowels). Accent the tops of the cake tiers with toasted coconut flakes.

This tangy delight is a vegan's fantasy come true. Finally, a curd you can eat! While egg yolks, sugar, butter, and lemon juice make up a classic lemon curd, in this version lemon juice and evaporated cane juice are the main ingredients, so it's extra lemony. Substitute lime juice for lime curd or orange juice for orange curd.

Lemon Curd

MAKES ABOUT 3 CUPS | 750 GRAMS

3 tablespoons cornstarch

1¼ cups | 296 ml fresh lemon juice
(or Pure Lemon from Lakewood Organic,
a great store-bought lemon juice)

1¼ cups | 350 grams evaporated cane juice

Grated zest of 1 lemon

¼ teaspoon fine sea salt

2 tablespoons soy or rice milk

2 tablespoons non-hydrogenated
palm shortening

① Place the cornstarch in a small bowl and set aside.

② In a small saucepan over medium heat, combine the lemon juice, evaporated cane juice, lemon zest, and salt. Cook, stirring, until the evaporated cane juice is dissolved.

③ Carefully pour a small amount of the hot liquid into the cornstarch. Stir thoroughly, and then add the cornstarch mixture back into the saucepan with the rest of the lemon juice mixture.

④ Add the soy milk to the saucepan. Slowly bring to a soft boil and cook, stirring constantly, until the mixture thickens, about 10 minutes.

⑤ Add the shortening and continue to cook, stirring constantly, for 10 to 15 minutes, until the mixture resembles a thick pudding.

⑥ Transfer the curd to a heatproof dish and cover the top with plastic wrap pressed directly on the surface of the curd to prevent a skin from forming. Let cool to room temperature before refrigerating.

⑦ Refrigerate for at least 2 hours before using. The curd can be refrigerated in an airtight container for up to 1 month.

Tarts are especially versatile desserts and offer variety when served as part of a multi-dessert table. Baked tart shells can be filled with just about anything, from icing to ganache to lemon curd, and effortlessly decorated with fresh or candied fruit. This tart dough can be used in any size tart pan, from tiny tartlet pans to 10-inch rounds, as well as rectangular tart pans. Grease and dust the tart pans with gluten-free flour to prevent the dough from sticking. If you don't have tart pans handy, small or large cupcake pans work really well as an alternative!

Sugar Tart Dough

MAKES ABOUT 28 OUNCES | 805 GRAMS,
ENOUGH FOR TWO 9-INCH ROUND TARTS OR FOUR DOZEN 2- TO 3-INCH TARTS

1 tablespoon golden flaxseed meal

3 tablespoons warm water

DRY INGREDIENTS

3 cups | 450 grams Lael Cakes
   Gluten-Free Flour (page 11)

1 cup | 210 grams evaporated cane juice

½ teaspoon baking powder

¼ teaspoon baking soda

¼ teaspoon fine sea salt

WET INGREDIENTS

½ cup | 120 ml safflower oil

1 cup | 147.5 ml vanilla soy or rice milk

½ teaspoon vanilla bean paste (or 1 vanilla
   bean pod or ¼ teaspoon vanilla extract)

① In a small bowl, combine the flaxseed meal and water. Set aside.

② In the bowl of a standing mixer with a paddle attachment, combine the gluten-free flour, evaporated cane juice, baking powder, baking soda, and salt. Mix on low speed to incorporate the ingredients.

③ In a separate bowl, combine the oil, soy milk, and vanilla. Add the flaxseed meal mixture.

④ With the mixer on low speed, slowly add the wet ingredients to the dry ingredients. Scrape down the side and bottom of the bowl and then raise the mixer speed to medium-high and beat for about 2 minutes, until all ingredients are just incorporated.

⑤ Transfer the dough and any crumbs in the mixer to a floured surface and knead until all ingredients are incorporated.

⑥ Wrap tightly in plastic wrap and refrigerate for 1 hour before using. Store in the refrigerator for up to 3 weeks or freeze for up to 6 months.

TO MAKE TART SHELLS:

① Divide the dough into two pieces. Work with one piece at a time, keeping one in the refrigerator when not in use.

② Preheat the oven to 350°F.

③ On a floured surface, roll the dough out into a circle about ⅛ inch thick, rotating continually to prevent sticking.

④ With a paring knife or a circle cutter, trim the dough into circles about 1 inch wider than the tart pans (you can use mini or standard cupcake pans if you don't have tarts pans for the smaller tarts shown in the dessert tables).

⑤ Gently lay the tart dough circles into the pans and press lightly on the sides. If the dough hangs over the edge of the pan, trim the excess dough from around the edge.

⑥ Bake small tart shells for 5 to 10 minutes, until golden brown and crisp. For larger tart shells, baking times will vary. Let cool completely before filling.

Candied Citrus

Candied citrus is an easy way to beautifully accent any cake or dessert! Start by making simple syrup: Combine 1 part evaporated cane juice and 1 part water in a saucepan and cook over medium heat for about 10 minutes, until the evaporated cane juice has dissolved and the solution is syrupy. Thinly slice the citrus (blood orange, grapefruit, kumquat, lemon, lime, and orange work great), then cook in the hot simple syrup over medium heat for about 10 minutes. Transfer to a baking sheet and bake at 235°F for 20 to 30 minutes, until the fruit is glistening and the texture becomes crisp. The larger the piece of fruit, the longer it will take to bake.

I have vivid memories of my great grandmother, Ma, twirling around her kitchen at the farmhouse in her apron, effortlessly whipping up desserts for special occasions. She always made simple but impressive desserts, an idea I carry with me to this day. There's nothing better than a recipe that has fewer than five ingredients. These versatile macaroons, which can be scooped to any size of your liking, can be served plain or embellished with chocolate: Drizzle with melted chocolate, or, for something extra special, make an imprint in the center while the macaroons are still warm, let cool, and then fill with Ganache (page 69).

Coconut Macaroons

MAKES 1–2 DOZEN, DEPENDING ON THE SIZE OF THE SCOOP

4 cups | 200 grams unsweetened
  coconut flakes

1 cup | 210 grams evaporated cane juice

2 cups | 500 ml water

1 teaspoon coconut flavor or extract

① Preheat the oven to 350°F.

② Place the coconut flakes in a large bowl and set aside.

③ Combine the evaporated cane juice and water in a saucepan over medium heat.

④ Cook, stirring occasionally, until the evaporated cane juice has dissolved and the mixture turns into a thick syrup. Stir in the coconut extract.

⑤ Remove from heat, pour over the coconut, and let sit for about 5 minutes.

⑥ Stir to combine. Use an ice cream scoop to shape the mixture into tightly packed balls. I like to use a 1-ounce scoop, but you can use any size. Place on a parchment-lined baking sheet, leaving about 1 inch between each ball.

⑦ Bake, rotating every 5 minutes, until the macaroons are lightly golden, 10 to 15 minutes.

⑧ Let cool completely before storing. Store, refrigerated, in an airtight container for up to 2 weeks.

I have a weakness for caramel. The flavor profile of this version has the best of all worlds—sweet, burnt, and salty! With the addition of coconut milk and shortening, this caramel has the consistency of a thick, decadent sauce. My all-time favorite way to use it is as a tart filling, topped with large flake sea salt. (Cue mouth water.) It can also be lightly drizzled over a cake, used as a coating for caramel apples, or even as a filling for cupcakes. However you use it, top it off with coarse sea salt for an extra sweet-and-salty twist.

Caramel Sauce

MAKES ABOUT 3 CUPS | 990 GRAMS

4 cups | 840 grams evaporated cane juice

1 cup | 250 ml water

½ cup | 120 ml agave nectar

1 cup | 235 ml coconut milk

¼ cup | 45.5 grams non-hydrogenated palm oil shortening

½ teaspoon sea salt

① Combine the evaporated cane juice, water, and agave in a medium saucepan. Stir lightly to incorporate. Make sure the sides of the pan are clean.

② Place the pan over high heat and cook until the mixture boils and starts to caramelize, about 20 minutes. Do not stir. Right when it turns dark golden brown, remove from the heat. Sugar burns very easily at this stage, so watch carefully!

③ Immediately, but slowly, stir in the coconut milk and shortening.

④ Stir in the sea salt and let cool completely before using.

⑤ To store, refrigerate in an airtight container for up to 3 months.

Resources

INGREDIENTS

ARROWHEAD MILLS
(gluten-free flours)
arrowheadmills.com

BARRY FARM FOODS
(gluten-free flours, sugars,
spices and herbs, leaveners,
and thickeners)
barryfarm.com

BEST FLAVORS
(oil-based flavorings, fruit and
vegetable powders)
bestflavors.com

BOB'S RED MILL
(gluten-free flours, sugars,
leaveners, thickeners)
bobsredmill.com

EDEN FOODS
(fruit juices, nondairy milks)
edenfoods.com

FRONTIER CO-OP
(thickeners, oil-based flavorings,
cacao nibs, carob powder,
cocoa powder)
frontiercoop.com

THE GLUTEN-FREE MALL
(fruit juices and purees,
gluten-free flours)
glutenfreemall.com

LAEL CAKES
(gluten-free flour mix)
laelcakes.com

NAVITAS NATURALS
(fruit and vegetable powders,
sugars, cacao nibs, cocoa
powder, chocolate chips)
navitasnaturals.com

NUTS.COM
(coconut flakes and chips, dried
fruit, nuts, fruit and vegetable
powders, herbs and spices,
gluten-free flours, leaveners,
thickeners, raw cocoa powder)

SINGING DOG VANILLA
(vanilla bean products)
singingdogvanilla.com

SPECTRUM
(plant-based fats, palm oil
shortening, vinegars)
spectrumorganics.com

WHOLESOME SWEETENERS
(sugars and sweeteners)
wholesomesweeteners.com

SUGAR SCULPTING AND DECORATING TOOLS

COLOR GARDEN
(plant-based liquid food coloring)
colorgarden.net

THE COMPLEAT SCULPTOR
(brushes, sculpting tools, Styrofoam shapes)
sculpt.com

GLOBAL SUGAR ART
(metallic powders, powder dyes, sculpting tools, molds, cutters, cake pans, sprinkles and dragées, piping bags and tips, cake boxes and boards, stencils)
globalsugarart.com

GUILDCRAFT FURNITURE
(Styrofoam shapes)
guildcraftfurniture.com

INDIA TREE
(natural food coloring, sprinkles)
indiatree.com

N.Y. CAKE
(metallic powders, powder dyes, sculpting tools, molds, cutters, cake pans, sprinkles and dragées, piping bags and tips, cake boxes and boards, stencils)
nycake.com

SCULPTOOLS STUDIO
(sculpting tools)
skulptools.com

SUGARCRAFT
(a variety of baking and decorating ingredients and materials)
sugarcraft.com

BAKING TOOLS

KEREKES
(cake pans, baking equipment, cake boards)
bakedeco.com

KITCHENKRAFTS
(pans, bakeware, measuring tools, cake boxes and boards)
kitchenkrafts.com

WEBSTAURANTSTORE.COM
(kitchen equipment and smallwares)

· · · · · · · · · · · · · · · · · ·

I'D LIKE TO GIVE ALL OF MY THANKS TO:

Carla Glasser, who first saw the potential in my work
and has guided me with her honesty and wit.

Stephanie Fletcher, for her brilliant editing.

Justin Schwartz and the phenomenal team at Houghton Mifflin,
for making my fantasy come to life!

Lauren Volo, my sister in creativity, who took the photographic imagery
far beyond anything I could have dreamed of.

Brita Olsen, for her hand in styling and lending irreplaceable props.

Liza Lubell, for friendship and flowers.

Rachel, my dearest friend, goddess, mentor, and the most amazing sister
I could have ever imagined being blessed with.

Mom and Dad, for guiding me to be the woman I am today and believing
in my every adventure. Not to mention passing along their amazing genes!

Mama Whipkey, for being my superhero and showing me
the path to a healthy lifestyle.

My grandmothers, who instilled my love of baking and the
memories of fresh cookies coming out of the oven.

· · · · · · · · · · · · · · · · · ·

Index

NOTE: Page references in *italics* indicate photographs